LIFE FROM
ELSEWHERE

LIFE FROM ELSEWHERE

JOURNEYS THROUGH WORLD LITERATURE

PUSHKIN PRESS

LONDON

Pushkin Press
71–75 Shelton Street
London WC2H 9JQ

Life from Elsewhere: Journeys Through World Literature first published in 2015

In partnership with English PEN, supported by Bloomberg, Arts Council England and ALCS.

0 0 1

ISBN 978 1 782271 89 5

Set in Monotype Baskerville 11.5 on 16 by Tetragon, London

Printed by CPI Group (UK) Ltd, Croydon, CRO 4YY

www.pushkinpress.com

CONTENTS

INTRODUCTION

AMIT CHAUDHURI

M Y PARENTS spoke with each other in Sylheti. They were both born in Sylhet, which had gone to East Pakistan upon partition, and they'd known each other since they were children. What they spoke was, admittedly, a gentrified version of this robust East Bengali dialect, often characterized (even by East Bengalis) as being, along with the dialect of Chittagong, near incomprehensible and slightly buffoonish. (It's worth recalling that the generic term for the East Bengali, *bangal*, also used to be synonymous with "villager" or "yokel".) Sylheti is a variation of the standard Bengali that emanates from Calcutta, and, to many, it's a comic variation. Besides, it is a language, as Marshall McLuhan would have put it, "without an army and a navy", though standard Bengali doesn't have an army and a navy either. What standard Bengali did have, for a number of historical reasons, was cultural prestige. A great-uncle on my father's side reportedly advised my parents against speaking in Sylheti with me (my father, by now, was working in Bombay), probably because of its low pedigree in the social world of languages: it was a language without a future, he told them. Given the considerable entrepreneurial skills of Bangladeshi Sylheti Muslims, who single-handedly invented "Indian cuisine" and "curry" in Britain, he was to be proved wrong, but I don't think he'd have cared anyway. My future was going to be forward-looking and cultured; Sylheti couldn't possibly play a part in it.

Nevertheless, I continue to hear that tongue being spoken, and I once absorbed stories about Sylhet—from my mother, mainly, but also my father and my maternal uncles. The comedic strain of much of this recounting was undeniable: it would have to do, for instance, with the hubris of cousins and cousins' imbecilic best friends who, while generally unable to conduct a conversation in uninflected Bengali, had ambitions—transformed as they were by Tagore and modern Bengali literature—to become poets. So much in Sylhet was, it seemed, the *bangal*'s daydream. And then there was the political history: partition, and the loss of home, memories that went back to partially noticed tensions and misunder-standings with Muslim friends who would turn against the narrator of the tale at the time of the referendum that decided Sylhet's future in 1947. One thing was clear: everything had happened in Sylhet. The upheavals of history had happened there; so had the newly minted magic of literature and the incursion of the songs of Tagore, Rajanikanta, D.L. Roy and Atul Prasad. Sylhet was the centre of the universe, if these reminiscences were to be trusted. It had the oiliest *hilsa* fish my mother had ever tasted; the most extravagant *paat shaak* greens. The *pithha* my mother's mother made were the most refined and delicate anywhere; this was borne out later by their reproduction in Bombay.

These memories could have added up to an account of a lost home, or a lost paradise or idyll, but they didn't. They could have been viewed through the lens of partition and exile, as the story of a continuing separation, but they weren't. Sylhet, being neither Calcutta nor Dhaka, could have been interpreted as a peripheral location, but it wasn't. In my relatives' narratives, it was, very simply, a centre. In other words, its appeal was neither personal nor immemorial; it was cultural and historical, animated by that moment to which those childhoods and that youth belonged. My relatives had been changed as well as made the people they were as a result of being situated in that town and in that history. For this reason, the division of the world into metropolitan centres and margins never quite rang true with me. Hardly anyone I met when I was growing up seemed to have actually known what it meant to live on the margins. They all seemed to have been located in the midst of history, wherever they came from.

What does it mean to be a "centre"? It doesn't entail transcending the local or even the provincial, as the example of Sylhet shows. Its self-sufficiency doesn't denote an independence from the outside world: where my parents and uncles were concerned, what we call the "international" was constantly impinging on their way of looking at things. But the "international" was most palpable in certain neighbourhoods and houses and conversations in Sylhet. To be in a centre meant *believing* you were in a centre; it meant to experience history as something you were being transformed by and might even contribute to. Much of this experience would happen in the head: in thoughts, speculations, longueurs, and in a form of immersion. This did not mean that this experience was less true than that of the centre, the city, in which the marks of metropolitan centrality were more overt. Nor did it mean that in the more canonical centres the experience of centrality was exclusively outward and visible, and unconnected to the daydream. All centres are to an important degree fictional and fictionalizing, in that they exist to some extent in the heads of people, in wishful thinking, and, as a result, are partly invisible. As the novelist and scientist Sunetra Gupta says about growing up in the Calcutta of the 1970s: "It is not a criticism that our love for the city was rooted neither in its history nor in its geography, for where it existed was in the life of the mind of its inhabitants." The greatest excitements of living in a centre are internal, invented and not easily accessible from the outside.

Just as the life of the centre is often covert, and connected to the daydream, the marks of whatever it is that makes a culture, place or person "international" are implicit. In Japan, in the twentieth century, we could assume that the suit—dark jacket and trousers and tie— was a mark of (for the want of a better descriptive term) Westernization. But for the Bengali bourgeois, the suit was a sign of mimicry, as were the use of English and of cutlery. The minority that took on these habits was mockingly referred to as *ingabanga* (the "Anglo-Bengalis"). In the *bhadralok*, the native Bengali bourgeoisie, one confronted a type of Europeanization much deeper than that in the *ingabanga*, precisely because their European eclecticism expressed itself as Bengaliness. The most obvious way it did this was in the dress of the *bhadralok*: the native *dhuti* and *panjabi*, immediately identifiable at the time with not just a locality or a city but with what Gupta calls "the life of the mind". To the outsider, the *bhadralok*'s Europeanness is hardly noticeable: his immersion is part of his invisibility. This question of invisibility then raises the question of what we understand—or notice—as being contemporary or immemorial, local or international, anywhere, whether in Calcutta or Japan or England.

My sense, increasingly, is that the twentieth century was made up not of peripheral locations (which people either departed, or remained in as provincials) and of canonical, acknowledged metropolises which many gravitated towards: it comprised innumerable centres.

All centres are, to a certain extent, invisible, because they're created most compellingly in the imagination; but some are invisible to a greater degree than others. Which is why it's such a surprise to realize, in retrospect, that certain places, like Sylhet, *were*, after all, invisible, though it hardly seemed so to those who lived there. The middle-class inhabitants of pre-partition Sylhet were aware of their, and their language's, distinctiveness as an eccentricity, while experiencing their location in all its urgency, plenitude and immediacy. *Other* places, whether those were London or Calcutta, felt curiously marginal. One has to respect this skewed vantage point as being not only real, but more true to what constitutes modernity than the accounts we have familiarized ourselves with and internalized. Our challenge is to recognize the invisible for what it is, and, through it, to try to access the different, interrelated, competing points of excitement that have made up our world.

THE DREAM
CALLED AFRICA

ALAIN MABANCKOU

I MADE A DECISION a long time ago not to shut myself in, to tune in to the sound and fury of the world, and never to take a rigid view of things. I didn't become a writer because I emigrated, but once I'd left it, I saw my country differently. In my early writings—all drafted in the Congo—I felt there were pieces missing; my characters were confined, stifled, they needed me to give them more space. Emigrating heightened the sense of unease which I've always believed is at the heart of all creative activity. You write because "something's not quite right", to try to move mountains or get an elephant through the eye of a needle. Writing grounds you; it's a cry in the dark, too, and the tilt of the ear to the horizon.

I was born in Africa, in Congo-Brazzaville, and spent much of my early life in France, before settling in the United States. The Congo is the base of my umbilical cord, France the adoptive land of my dreams, and America the place from which I look back on the trail I've left behind me. These three geographical places are now fused, and sometimes I forget which continent I went to bed in, which one I'm in as I write.

I've been to so many towns, and loved them all. I'm amazed by all these places that are nothing like where I grew up. I arrive with a heart that's light, and a mind free of thoughts of any kind. The true emigrant does not export his customs or tastes, seeking to impose them on the host country. It's the contrast between the place where we live and our "natural milieu" that brings childhood images back up to the surface, the street noises, the suffering, the joy of our own people. The tornado season reminds you of the virtues of a clear blue sky, the swoop of a free-flying bird and the explosion of a scent you can't quite name, until one day you remember it also grows round the back of your father's hut.

With the proliferation of means of communication we've created new regions, networks shooting off throughout the world. "Rome is no longer in Rome", the writer becomes a migratory bird, who remembers the country he came from, but chooses to stay and sing on the branch where he's perched. Do the songs of these migratory birds still come under the banner of their national literature? I'm not sure they do, any more than I believe literature can be contained within specific borders. I wouldn't mind where I lived, provided it sheltered my dreams and let me reinvent my own world. I am both of these things: writer and migratory bird.

My concept of *identity* goes far beyond notions of *territory* or *blood*. I am nourished by each one of my encounters. It would be futile to stick merely to one's own patch, ignoring the endless interactions and consequent complexity of this new era in which we are all connected in ways that have nothing to do with geography.

In America I have often come across French people who considered me *truly* their compatriot, as though away from home, irrespective of racial origins, the French were prepared to broaden their sense of citizenship. As though a clearer definition of nationhood might be reached by leaving our homeland and meeting afresh somewhere where our culture can finally become the substantial link between us.

Just as we now need to reconsider what we mean by *territory*, we also need to re-examine the term *identity*. We should really look back at the origins of the word to remind ourselves of the extent to which the fearmongers have managed to transform a fluid idea into an ideology which is both static and suicidal for a nation. In the first instance identity derives from the self, the "I", the existence of an individual within society. It is what makes an individual or a group particular and singular. Just as an individual has an identity card, a group might have one too. But what features would we register on the identity card of a group? Identity is a statement not of what we are but of what we might become through intersection and exchange, through friction and migration, in an era which looks set to become that of the utmost complexity for the human race. In this respect, as an African, I no longer consider my continent as a land apart. Africa is no longer just in Africa. As they disperse throughout the world, Africans create other "Africas" and embark on new adventures, which may considerably enhance the cultural standing of the black continent. The black diaspora thus becomes a kind of "mobile Africa", a platform for African cultures. It is the birth of a new identity, not necessarily attached to Mother Africa, but with an autonomy of its own.

What is the nature of the connection, then, between Africans born in Europe and those who remain in Africa? They are two contradictory, and occasionally conflicting cultures, because they do not share the same vision of Africa, because Africa is a *dream* for some and a *reality* for others. An African born outside the African continent may well have little sense of connection to the Africa of his ancestors, which feels remote, distorted by news reports which reflect back an image of a land in the constant throes of tragedy and incapable of exploiting its immense riches. Equally, this same African, born outside the continent, is not recognized in his or her country of adoption, where the immigration laws and the policies of European governments grow increasingly inflexible. He doesn't belong "back there", but is not quite accepted "here" either. How will he react? What he needs is a way to express his condition, and what we are seeing is the emergence of an African "subculture".

The Africans of the diaspora are certainly aware of their attachment to Africa, but they mythologize the continent, and turn increasingly to black American culture, to which they feel closer. Perhaps we should also remember that black Americans—who chose to be called "African Americans"—also mythologize the black continent. African cultures survive, but in somewhat utopian form, based on an idea we have of the black continent. More often than not, when a diasporan black returns to Africa, he—or she—experiences a sense of total disconnection. They come face to face with a world quite unlike what they imagined. We need only consider, for example, the relationships between African Africans, black Americans and other people of black origin. Their mutual incomprehension results from the difficulty of defining what might be meant by "African identity", simply because no such thing exists— or ever could exist. Because this identity is the sum of the experience of black people all over the world. The African living in Africa encounters quite different situations to those of an African living in Europe, and black Americans have a history which an African from Africa could never understand. The coloured American has been subjected to migration by deed of history: the slave trade. He has had to fight for decades for his civil rights and for recognition as a citizen of the United States. The "continental" African, on the other hand, struggles against the dictatorial regime of his country, with famine, with the consequences of underdevelopment, while the European African is constantly questioning the real nature of his condition.

Seen from this angle, globalization requires us to see ourselves as one element in a much larger, more complex culture which absorbs our individual experience and multifarious encounters. And as we come to assess the consequences of globalization, it should not surprise us to find black Africa pushed into the background, even though migration lies at the heart of its culture, and though courtesy and hospitality have long been the proudest boasts of the black continent...

When people ask me about the influence of emigration on my writing, I find it impossible to give a precise or definitive answer. Probably because I become increasingly convinced that changing places and crossing borders feeds my anxieties and contributes to the creation of an imaginary country, a place that finally begins to look something like where I first came from, the Congo Republic...

Translated by Helen Stevenson

A COMPASS WITH
TWO SOUTHS

ANDRÉS NEUMAN

T HEY SAY you never forget the south. But what happens to memory when you have two souths? The best thing about not being born in Granada is that one day, as a South American boy, I had the chance to feel I was *arriving* in Granada. Today, almost twenty-five years later, I'm still living in Andalusia: in the south of the south of Europe.

When we were children, my brother and I felt as if we were living in a Julio Cortázar story, where there is often a door that opens onto another reality. Inside our house, within the four walls of our family microclimate, we were in Argentina. But as soon as the door was opened, we went out to play in Spain. The frontier between the two countries was no more than a doorknob. As I write now, I have that same sensation.

I think my impulses to write come mainly from a sense of perplexity towards my mother tongue. Emigration produced an intimate conflict with my own language. To be able to communicate with my new schoolmates in Granada, I spent a couple of terms mentally translating from Argentine Spanish to peninsular Spanish: I was looking for equivalences, comparing pronunciations, thinking every word from both sides. At first, this exercise cost me a great effort. After a while, however, it became a spontaneous reaction. It's as though my right ear could hear the language of one shore, my left ear that of the other shore, while my mouth tried to articulate what both of them had perceived. Nowadays I am no longer capable of thinking or writing without submitting everything I say to a kind of forked listening, possibly something akin to the bewilderment of a passenger in transit.

*

Granada faces a daily paradox. Traditionalist, centuries old, caught up in its own legend, its streets are however constantly invaded by hordes of polyglot tourists and drunken students (forgive my stating the obvious). It can seem as if time has stopped for the city, and yet it is filled with travellers in transit. Hardly any tourist stays more than one or two days, hardly any students stay on here after they have graduated. This fugitive destiny gives the city a certain liquid quality that modifies its tendency to stasis. In this it is similar to the architecture of the Alhambra.

In recent decades, Andalusia has undergone a rapid transformation. On the way, it has often had to face a cultural dilemma: how to modernize without defrauding the tourist? How to reshape the identity of somewhere that millions of visitors from the world over come to see thinking only of bullfights, sun and siesta? Apart from idyllic villages, flamenco and home cooking, Andalusia boasts countless artists still alive, in addition to Picasso; an intense university life; a growing scientific presence (Granada's Science Park is among the best in Europe); classical orchestras; and even good football. That is possibly why one of the biggest challenges Andalusia faces is to make its own identity more foreign.

Despite its hackneyed folkloric image, the lands of Andalusia do not offer a single aesthetic, let alone a unified spirit, whatever on earth that might mean. As a region of poor emigrants, African immigrants and adventurers to the Indies, as well as a melting pot of races for more than a thousand years, Andalusia not only receives you, but even more importantly allows you to remain a foreigner. I think this is the best thing one can say of anywhere.

*

The literary canon appears to contain two paradigms for a Latin American author living in another country: exile from dictatorship or economic migration. My family situation doesn't fit either of these categories. My parents' emigration from Argentina did have a political overtone, as they decided to leave when former president

Menem pardoned the military leaders responsible for the dictatorship and genocide from 1976 to 1983, but no one expelled them or persecuted them, as had happened with my two uncles and aunts, as well as many thousands of other Argentine families. Nor did I have to leave for strictly professional or economic reasons, still less to get on in the literary world: I was simply a young boy who travelled with his parents as part of their luggage.

Like a piece of luggage lost in an unfamiliar airport, our homeland is a certainty which in fact depends on circumstances. For anyone who thinks it implies a specific country, spending half your life in another one creates a huge question mark. For anyone who thinks our true homeland is our childhood, it's enough to remind them that there are events that can split a childhood in two: a war, a death, exile. As a final proof of patriotism, it's often insisted that a writer's homeland is his or her language. But if this were the case, the work of those authors who changed the language they wrote in could not be explained.

I'm thinking for example of Nabokov, who following his Russian, tsarist education went on to revolutionize English prose. Or Beckett, as Irish as his master Joyce, who later became part of the French avant-garde. Or Cioran, whose originality of thought seems to me impossible to separate from his transfer from Romanian to French: a writer from the margins adopting a central language. Or the Polish Conrad, whose particular observation of mankind was as close and meticulous as was his learning of the English language. Or Rodolfo Wilcock, who can be studied as an Argentine writer in Italian. Or Hector Bianciotti, who adopted French and eventually became a member of the French Academy, only to spend all his time writing about his Argentine childhood. Or another writer I admire, Charles Simić, whose poems steeped in North American orality reflect his Balkan origin. Or the strange poet Alfredo Gangotena, who was born in Quito but emigrated to Paris. He wrote the greater part of his work in French, and continued to do so after returning to his native Ecuador. One of his poems opens with an untranslatable rhyme: "*J'apprends la grammaire / de ma pensée solitaire.*" (I learn the grammar / of my solitary thought.) In every poem, to some extent, grammar and solitude rhyme.

Many years after his death, Gangotena was finally translated into Spanish. To be translated into one's own mother tongue! Perhaps something similar happens to a writer whenever a compatriot reads him.

*

Literature does not really have a mother tongue. Writing translates words into a different language, whose grammar is constantly a matter of debate. The strangeness that a poem stammers in every syllable somehow reproduces the experience of the foreigner when he is trying to pronounce another tongue. In both cases, the point of departure is the feeling of distance with regard to language. Not knowing exactly how to say what we are saying.

If poetry and translation are closely connected, this is not simply because many poets work as translators. It is more because, deep down, every poem sets up a silent translation mechanism. A state of suspicion towards language. Translators need to have doubts about every word, just as poets do. To the point that foreignness ends up invading their own linguistic homeland. Like someone spending the night in a hotel in their own city.

When a book is translated, its author—if he or she has the good luck and bad taste to be still alive—not only witnesses a transfer, but also a revelation. He learns what his book is capable of saying, or what it might have said. It's often claimed that a poor translation can ruin a masterpiece. But what is not so often stated is that good translators can broaden and improve any text. In this sense, a translator is simply a super-reader. In other words, a reader with the ability to rewrite. That is why I never entirely expect a translator to respect me, or a reader to understand me. What I really want is for both of them to invade me, transcend me, to give me their passport.

*

There are a couple of expressions that are very common in Buenos Aires that have always surprised me: the way *exterior* refers to any country that is not Argentina, and the way *interior* is used to refer to any city that is not Buenos Aires. Beyond the geographical, these spatial terms suggest a binary way of understanding how we belong to a nation. *In or out.* Given the huge increase in migratory flows over the past few decades, this characterization may already have started to become obsolete.

Nowadays there are many third realities and frontier identities. That is true for the hundreds of thousands of Latin American families living in Spain, where they have became mixed, and their memory, language and emotions have become hybrid. Can it be said that this phenomenon is *exterior* to the culture and history of their native lands? Many of these immigrants have not only mixed with their Spanish neighbours, but also have children born there. This will necessarily mean a reformulation of national identity on both shores: there are increasing numbers of Spaniards brought up by Latin American families; more and more native Latin Americans who have grown up in Spain. There is something absurd about asking them what they are, which side they come from, which shore they prefer to give up. Like it or not, they are frontier citizens.

*

The novelist José Donoso, who lived in both Chile and Europe as Roberto Bolaño did, once declared that the price of freedom is not to belong anywhere. On the one hand, the emigrant knows the freedom of distance, of not having to live every day with the national culture he was brought up in. On the other hand, that very same distance creates a difficulty for him or her to put down roots in the new place, and even to return to his or her birthplace. The emigrant gains exactly what he loses: the sense of belonging. Or, to put it another way, the sense of a homeland as something natural. Thus, the homeland can become an imaginary quest, a future literary construction, an intimate fiction. I like to remember Simone Weil's advice about inhabiting a city: "put down roots in the absence of place." I feel close to this idea of residing without a central focus, this founding of a nomad territory. And I believe that literature can be the guide on this journey. The mother without a homeland.

My idea of foreignness then has less to do with being outside a place than with the idea of a continuous frontier. With that meeting point where something becomes double. With the door linking two houses. That is why I feel close to the double-headed sensibility of second generations, those children of migrants who have learned one culture in their homes and another out in the street, customs from their parents, and different ones from the people around them; one collective memory from their family and another from their friends or partners.

Possibly the German poet Novalis was right, and literature is "a desire to feel at home everywhere". Or the opposite: why not live and write with the same feeling of strangeness everywhere, even in our own supposed homeland? As one of Schubert's *lieder* has it: "as a foreigner I come, / as a foreigner I go." There is room for all of us on the frontier, but the frontier should not belong to anyone.

Translated by Nick Caistor

TO UNDERSTAND
A CULTURE IS
DIFFICULT, BUT...

CHAN KOONCHUNG

T O UNDERSTAND A CULTURE is difficult, even for a person embedded in that culture.

To understand another culture is more difficult, if not impossible. But giving up is not an option. As the always perceptive Chinese novelist Chang Ailing once said: "Only with understanding will there be empathy." This is a conundrum faced by our densely layered, multi-cultural world.

However, the Sisyphean effort of mundane cultural exchanges may well be the only escape route out of the conundrum, even if we enter into the exchanges with our prejudices already in place: in spite of our intention to be open-minded, we may inevitably carry certain ethno-centric pre-conceptions or culturally acquired attitudes when we encounter another culture. But this should not prevent us from reaching out... I shall explain later.

Let's think about China for a moment.

As a Sinophone writer, I am very aware that no one, Chinese included, can explain in a nutshell what China is, for three broad reasons. First, only tourists would go to a high deck to have a panoramic scenic view and then leave with a feel-good impression that they already have a sense of the place. To make things more complicated, in reality there is no high, panoramic viewing deck, or an Archimedean privileged point, when it comes to understanding a culture.

Second, not only is China huge and multifarious, but the civilization has been incessantly hybridized and has mutated through the centuries, and its territorial reach varied like waves of successive high tides and low tides, with two tidal waves of total submersion when the then antebellum China was only a fraction of the immense Mongol and Manchu empires.

Third, misdiagnoses and stereotyping abound when talking about China. Early Enlightenment thinkers such as Voltaire praised the secular governance in traditional Chinese society, while later European opinions cast China in a negative light: isolation, backwardness, incompetence, hostility to innovation, and so on. Views from China itself could be equally misleading. Emperor Qianlong's famous 1793 assertion to a British royal convoy that "we have no need for (English) manufactures" was taken at face value by many Chinese, though in fact the empire's tremendously successful expansion by Qianlong and his predecessors was partly facilitated by new weaponry and scientific knowledge from the West transmitted with the help of Jesuit priests.

There can be no one "emic" (insider) view or one "etic" (outside or universal) view on China that can claim to be the only correct view. China is always Chinas in plurality—you will have to ask which China and when. There is no pure Chineseness just as there can be no essential Englishness. When it comes to describing a different culture, one must avoid the temptation of over-simplified assertions, or seeing things as dichotomous—that is, in black and white, or as good or bad.

Anyone who has more than a little knowledge about China would qualify whatever one says, lest one be like blind men describing an elephant. American philosopher A.N. Whitehead would call this kind of common and often innocuous over-blowing of partial truths a "fallacy of misplaced concreteness". Whatever China is today, it is the result of aeons of myriad cultural exchanges with others, forced or otherwise.

Cultural exchanges, however frustrating, actually made the world as we know it today. Take the much publicized Silk Road for instance. The term was coined by a German geographer in the late nineteenth century. It was a misnomer and had not been used by locals before. There was never a discernible road, but a patchwork of drifting trails within central Eurasia, marked by a constellation of oasis towns of mainly agricultural set-tlements. It was not a one-way trade, sending Chinese silk to the West: silk was only one among other, probably more important two-way trading goods that included chemicals, dyes, spices, metals, leather, glass, paper and, above all, cultural-specific knowledge. China's main trading partner was never Rome, as the legend went, but Samarkand in today's Uzbekistan, on the eastern edge of the Iranian world. The most recent research shows that the trading volume, mostly relayed between desolate local settlements, was usually small.

But these slow-moving exchanges made a huge difference to the world. To name two: religion and paper. Buddhism reached China from India before the first century and transformed later Chinese civilization. Manichaeism, Zoroastrianism, Eastern Christianity and, later, Islam travelled similarly and made their impacts there. Paper moved out of China overland in the eighth century, eventually reaching Europe via the Islamic lands of Sicily and Spain. Denizens north of the Alps made their own paper only in the late fourteenth century, but that made a big difference to subsequent transmission of knowledge which would in turn change the world.

Traditional empires were multi-ethnic, breaking down tribal territorial boundaries and often inadvertently promoting cultural exchanges. It could be "hegemonic", with the empires' core cultures mimicked by their subordinate peoples. But again the traffic could be in the other direction. The Mongol court, for instance, was known for attracting the service of artisans and technicians of different ethnicities from different parts of Eurasia, as Marco Polo would testify in the fourteenth century.

As the idea of the nation state was introduced in the seventeenth century and more broadly accepted after the Second World War, nation-building became a major preoccupation for many newly established countries, often too impatiently pursuing the ideal of "one nation, one state". But even the most ethnically homogenized countries like Korea and Japan have ethnic minorities, and any project of making "one nation, one state" through cultural homogenization, not to mention ethnic cleansing, would breed intra-cultural tension, ethnic conflicts and unacceptable human suffering.

Most nation states have to deal with a difficult choice between multiculturalism and assimilation, between particularism and universalism. Is there a middle way that embraces both respectful tolerance of cultural difference and genuine interest in promoting cultural exchanges in the process of nation-building?

Can one appreciate that one's own country is amazingly unique without being chauvinistic or self-centred, and realize that other countries are equally exceptional and worthy of fuller understanding, in our common pursuit of building an international community?

As globalization progresses and migration, refugees and mixed marriages become more common, today's world is irreversibly both mixed and bundled together. We know we are all among strangers, some more strange than others.

If we withdraw into ourselves and refuse to reach out, we will all end up living in our own ghettos.

I am of the opinion that one may never hope to understand other cultures fully, but that doesn't mean that we shouldn't try. So, even a dummy guide to China is a good place to start, while keeping in mind its inadequacy. After all it is the very gesture of trying to reach out that counts.

Having travelled a fair part of the globe, I would say the denizens of China are quite open to the outside world. Thousands of books are translated into Chinese and hundreds of international scholarly seminars are hosted by China every year. China is a major market for entertainment products from Korea, Japan, Europe, the United Kingdom and the United States. As China becomes more affluent, Chinese of all ages are becoming enthusiastic tourists willing to venture out into different parts of the world. In comparison, I have found North Americans less interested in overseas travel and foreign cultures than Chinese.

For a country like China, cultural exchanges have now become vibrant and commonplace. One may be dismayed at the quality of the exchanges, or be disappointed by the censorship of certain exchanges, but the fact is that China is very much investing in cultural exchanges, especially when compared with some rich European countries. That bodes well for both China and the world.

But that doesn't mean most Chinese are no longer culturally chauvinistic, or the majority is not nationalistic or even racist despite being more cosmopolitan, or the illiberal party state no longer jealously guards its often xenophobic ideological positions.

All I'm trying to say is: cultural exchange is messy. It is often one step forward and two steps backward. During the process, we could all be accused of being Eurocentric or Sinocentric, orientalists or occidentalists, neocolonialists or paranoid nativists, and we often feel that other people have failed to understand us. For instance, it is quite common for Chinese people to openly aver that foreigners can never understand China. I am sure the reverse is also true. But meanwhile, most people appreciate outsiders who make an effort to understand and befriend them. So the point about goodwill cultural exchanges has less to do with whether one could or should fully understand other cultures, but is more about our common desire to reach out, our modicum of effort to open up ourselves, and indeed to show goodwill to others, that gives a glimmer of hope to our confused world. That, incidentally, could change the world.

LILY

AYELET GUNDAR-GOSHEN

I N THIS CITY, the sun set two hours too early and morning arrived an hour too late, but that was bearable. What wasn't bearable was the smell. The lack of it. In his city, the air and the sea embraced each other, intertwined like a man and woman who have only just met and still want very much to do it. In this city, the air and the sea were like a man and a woman after an ugly fight, distant and hostile. He had actually been happy when they invited him to come here. He saw the city and the sea on the Internet site, and though it wasn't his city or his sea, there was still something in the familiar combination of the two that made him feel he would be comfortable there. That was before he knew about the sun setting too early and the lack of smell. It was possible to get used to the sun. You switched on the light in your room or turned the hands of the clock two hours forward, as if with two circular sweeps you could really hop continents, seas and hours. But the air here had no smell, and air is everything. He counted the hours until he could go home.

At six in the evening, he put on his best jacket and his best smile, which was folded in the pocket of his best jacket, and headed for the conference hall. The hotel reception clerk had drawn him a map earlier and he walked there without losing his way even once. He was proud of his navigational skills and disappointed by the flat, boring city that didn't have even a single, hidden wrinkle to suddenly divert a person from his course. The presenter welcomed him with an intimate handshake, whispered in his ear that she felt his book had been written especially for her, then blushed as if she knew she had said too much about herself and too little about the book, and with a brusque, almost angry movement, thrust the unfamiliar copy into his hand and said—*These are the passages I'm planning to read.* He opened the book which, though it bore his name, contained not a single word he could read, and stared at the passages marked with a yellow highlighter pen. He could easily have asked her to tell him what she had chosen. Her English was good enough to answer him. But the writer had spent the day immersed in a language that was not his, in interviews and meetings with readers and a brief visit to the municipal museum, and though he spoke English quite well, he felt a bit fatigued, as if he had been swimming with all his clothes on. He preferred to guess—looked at the woman opposite him and tried to imagine which, of all the lines he had written, she had liked well enough to colour yellow and read in front of the audience. And she, perhaps sensing his scrutinizing glance, said—*And most of all, I liked Lily.*

That was strange because the writer had never written about any Lily. He was certain of that. He had written about Moshe and Avi and Shelly, but not about Lily. The anger now crawled in his throat like a centipede. It was clear that the woman standing before him had not bothered to read his book. She had curled her hair and carefully chosen a blouse for the occasion, but she had not bothered to read his book. Or perhaps (and here he suddenly felt sorry for her, noticing the price tag protruding from her blouse, revealing how excited she had been when she left her home), perhaps she had read it and was simply confused. Lily and Shelly weren't such different names, and maybe in her language they were the same. He was still deciding whether to be angry or forgiving when she began pulling him towards the stage. The audience was already seated, and in countries like this, they don't keep people waiting. In his city, a ten-minute wait was not a big deal. Not only didn't people get angry about it, they enjoyed it, relishing the extra minutes the way children delight in snatching crumbs from a cake. But here the people glared at him—he had already squandered two minutes of their time, and one day, when their final moment came, they would remember clearly that they could have had two more minutes to live if that uncouth writer from the Levant had not stolen them. The last whisperers in the audience grew silent and the presenter began to speak. First she introduced him. He understood that from the rules of protocol and also from the looks she sent him at the end of each sentence, as if seeking confirmation. Here and there he recognized a word from his CV—university, Tel Aviv—and he thought that she had also awarded him, mistakenly, the rank of professor. Then she began to speak about the book. He understood that from the way she waved her hand at the cover in the foreign language, stroking it again and again in a way that did not leave his body indifferent. When he'd met her at the entrance to the conference hall, he thought she had a washed-out look, the sort of woman who, like a terminally ill patient, is kept alive only by artificial means. Now, speaking in her own language, she was suddenly animated by a certain charm that the English had blocked, and when she finally began to read from the book, the writer was already convinced that the flush he now saw on her cheeks came from an internal flame, not from externally applied blush. She began reading, and he fought against the urge to scan the faces of the audience to see their reactions to his words which now, in translation, were utterly foreign to him. Instead of looking at the audience, he stared into space with an expression that he hoped would appear to be full of meaning and restrained dignity. He was indeed in need of all the restrained dignity he could muster when, a moment later, he heard the name Lily.

Horrified, the writer listened intently to the rest of the paragraph. Present were Moshe and Avi and Shelly, all the people he himself had invited to be in his book. But there was also Lily. Her name appeared every few lines, rising above the other words that were in a language he did not understand. It was inconceivable. Here he was, sitting in a conference hall in a foreign city at his book launch, and some Lily was traipsing through his novel, uninvited, but definitely present, so much so that this woman, with her curled hair and new blouse, preferred her to the legal residents of the book. It was infuriating. It was inconceivable.

Suddenly the writer realized that he knew exactly who was responsible: Lily Sigalovitch, who had translated his book into this cold European language. A slender bespectacled young woman with a fig-red mouth whose perfection in the middle of her face merely emphasized the ordinariness of the features surrounding it. The writer had met her only once, at the conclusion of a conference at the museum. He was certain that she had come to thank him for his fascinating lecture, so he was somewhat disappointed when, instead of praising his lecture, she introduced herself as his translator. Several moments later, a number of enthusiastic members of the audience had gathered, eager to express their admiration, but Lily Sigalovitch did not let him go, saying she wanted to take the opportunity to talk to him about the novel, about his male point of view. The writer, barely able to hide his impatience in any case, detected a note of criticism in her words. One newspaper had already called him *phallocentric*, and also, *one of the guys*. They suggested that the book would have been much better with a strong female character in it. It was one thing to read such nonsense in a newspaper, but to hear that drivel from a woman who translated into some godforsaken language? He suggested they speak another time, and turned away from her even before she had time to ask for his address. After that encounter, she'd called him twice—the publisher had given her his number—and he'd spoken to her briefly, promising to get back to her, which he never did. In fact, he'd forgotten her completely—her mousey appearance, the fig-mouth whose beauty mocked the face it was stuck in, even her name—until this very moment.

Beside him on the stage, the presenter once again said the name Lily with the joy people feel when they read a favourite passage in a novel. Listening to her, he recalled how surprised he had been at the success of the book in this country. It hadn't been that successful anywhere else. The reviews at home were lukewarm. The ones abroad were even cooler. If his previous books hadn't done so well, it was doubtful that anyone would have bothered to translate it. And in this country—enormous success. Reviewers raved. Readers shook his hand, their eyes moist. And now he suddenly knew that it was because of her. Because of Lily Sigalovitch. His anger turned to bafflement—what had she done to his story? What secret ingredient had she added that made it all work? He answered the presenter's questions like an automaton, signed books in Hebrew, as usual, and knew that he would never know what there was in his book that made these people swarm around him this way. At the first opportunity, he slipped out of the hall. The air outside punched him with an icy fist.

Translated by Sondra Silverston

DIVISIONS OR UNITY?
ART AND THE REALITY
BEHIND THE STEREOTYPE

SAMAR YAZBEK

A RT IS NOT SOMETHING pure and inviolable; it is not impervious to divisions and schisms. Certainly we wish it to be, when we see it as a universal human language with the potential to liberate us from the cycle of violence along which trudges all human life, for all its diversity and variety. Predicated on double standards, and recurring in ever new guises and disguises, this violence is kept alive by politics and the media in line with the strategic and economic gains to be won in these never-ending conflicts.

To put it another way, art is indeed prone to divisive manipulation: not so much in its definition as an aesthetic act, but when used as a tool of media endorsement, of propaganda, of consolidating rigid, preconceived ideas. In its purest form, art should resist this with aesthetic independence and a focus on humanity and human concerns free from the constraints of religion, race or nationality.

Art poses questions; it forces a head-on confrontation with humanity. In a sense it humanizes all that is ugly and appalling within us by exposing it and opening it up to examination. Art approaches its subject from another perspective, breaking down the stereotype—be it that of the savage, backward "other" or the malevolent invader—into the minutiae of human life, creating a contrast between the version of reality that is manufactured for the benefit of political agendas and the real, living people who are trampled underfoot by both of these fabricated preconceptions. Looking at the people who live in a country like Syria in a humane way and hearing the details of their lives, seeing them as individuals with complex circumstances and tragic tales to tell—all of this is part of the process of trying to understand, of unravelling and dismantling society, of digging deep into its strata as a route to understanding.

What art does is make us look into each other's eyes and into the eyes of those who are portrayed as our enemies, transforming them into human beings. Art puts them on an equal footing with us. It deprives them of the perception that has traditionally been assumed in the collective consciousness, which sees them as a cohesive, homogenous bloc of people, which presupposes hostility and specific modes of behaviour. These assumptions are what form the roots of the growing racism and xenophobia around the world.

A novel can dismantle the world, not in a linguistic or philosophical sense, but in a way that transforms it into a spectrum of parallel lives. By painting a detailed portrait, a fictional narrative presents another perspective on the world, a deep and personal one where we lift the veil from the faces of real people, genuine faces that have not been manufactured by TV or social media. Literature, in all its forms, proposes aesthetic ways to take things apart and examine them, no matter how unsightly the subject matter. This is the basic code that gives literature the ability to enact change, as well as to preserve the memory of history. I am keenly aware of literature's capacity for this, as a novelist, journalist and activist, where I am constantly shifting between various levels of cultural and political discourse across a number of countries, each of them relating in a way which is hostile to another. And navigating between these countries has made me realize the challenges: it has made me recognize the deep chasm between populations—and I say "populations", not governments, because the cognitive and cultural identities formed by these populations are in large part a reaction to the actions of their governments. So, with these global prejudices on the one hand, bolstered by neo-capitalism as it pursues its interests throughout the world, and with these fiery, fanatical religious and nationalist groups on the other hand, who are perceived through the prism of the growing enmity between Islam and the West, how then can we think about art? Surely we cannot see it in isolation from this mounting hostility, mistrust and fear between the two camps? This is a conundrum which keeps me awake at night.

Given the current turmoil in the Arab world, there is a real appetite for a new form of misanthropy and misunderstanding to sow division and keep apart the two distinct worlds. For it would seem that the global Cold War between the two camps led by the former Soviet Union and the US, which culminated in the break-up of the Soviet superpower, needs a new outlet to continue in this era, in an updated format. There needs to be an enemy, and this "other"—this apocryphal, trumped-up nemesis which we must struggle to defeat—needs to exist for eternity. And it is also this "other" which we see reflected in literature and art. With the great enemy of the West emerging in an alarming, dangerous and terrifying form in the guise of Islamic extremism and most recently the Islamist militant group Daesh, or ISIS, what can art hope to achieve as a universal language within this disastrous war that is unfurling between the West and Islam? Little by little the scale of this conflict is becoming apparent, but the question already looms large: what power will existing art forms have to shatter received perceptions, as we stand now on the threshold of a new era of covert, convoluted wars spiralling ever outwards, offering ever new ways for the North West to impose authority and dependency on the South, with its abject poverty and its burden of dictatorships and religious extremism? Is there a role here for art as a universal language? And where can we squeeze literature into all of this?

Literature offers us a parallel universe which sits alongside the one we inhabit, but this version of reality is also often the more enduring one. In a work of fiction, history is endowed with a human side, imbued with the memory of victims. In literature we can disentangle the intricate relationships between people; we can turn vague, murky stereotypes, which the masters of the new world so love to exploit, into rounded, well-defined portraits. When a novel describes how people fall victim to double standards, how they are manipulated and their human dignity is worn away, we see them stripped bare. By this I mean that we see a stark exposition of the ugliness deep within us, our shameful choices and our indecision, our fear and our confusion. Literature lays bare our magnanimity and our malevolence. Rather than reducing people to clichéd tools of propaganda, if a fictional narrative can flesh out two-dimensional tropes into credible, lifelike human characters, then these people are brought into the real world of the reader.

Imagine, for example, a novel about a woman living in Syria now: as a Muslim, we might assume that she wears a veil in accordance with the traditions and customs of her society, and we'll assume that she lives in an area still controlled by the Assad regime. As the protagonist, we learn about the challenges she faces, the fears and anxieties that fill her daily life. The more we read, the more we see traditional stereotypes being picked apart—for example, the entrenched rhetoric about Sunnis and Alawites, established and perpetuated by the regimes of Hafez al-Assad and his son Bashar. Imagine she lives in the city, not in the countryside—an important distinction, because of the widespread impoverishment of rural Syria—and her home is in the city centre, as opposed to the poor suburbs of Damascus. This novel then goes on to describe her female neighbour who has lived alongside her for decades and who belongs to another religious denomination. The narrative would speak of the fear this neighbour now feels as a Sunni: fear that now pushes her door firmly closed after all this time as neighbours. We then delve closer into the deep, enduring friendship between these two neighbours, which has been tested and distorted over the last four years. We learn that the two women have children who have grown up together as if they were one family, who have eaten and travelled together, but then with the beginning of the revolution in 2011, the cracks start to show. One of the sons joins the Syrian army, while another signs up to the revolution. When another son is arrested, and is tortured and killed at the hands of his torturers, his brother joins the ranks of the revolutionary Free Army. The women's sons disappear, one after another. Both women have a family and a history and traditions which they cannot escape from, and while their husbands are just about neutral, with time this neutrality disappears too. But what can you say when you have lived together for so many years as sisters?

All of this represents the process of dissecting the stereotype of the "other"—here at a local level—by transforming these clichés into characters of flesh and blood. How can we ever forget these people when we, as readers, are the ones responsible for bringing them to life? When, through the act of reading, we have set their stories into motion, when we have articulated their pain and how they've been stripped of their past by the war-torn society into which post-revolutionary Syria has descended? By portraying the lives of these two women in minute detail, the novel helps us transform their pain into a multidimensional representation of their tragic reality, as well as turning you, the reader, into a voyeuristic spectator behind the scenes, a privileged witness to the hidden reality which is of so little concern to the media outlets, the politicians and the arms traders—the shady apparatus of war. We Syrians are here, and if we can give readers easier access to our literature, then we can welcome them into our homes, take them behind closed doors into our real lives, to help them see that we are just human beings, ordinary people who desire only justice, real people who are dying while the world watches on in apathy. We are human beings, condemned by the laws of military might and international self-interest. You might, dear reader, find that the grandiose words used to create sensational and enticing newspaper headlines are not in fact appropriate for this tragedy which has engulfed the Syrians since they requested freedom and democracy, while the international community has stood idly by, watching the carnage: the endless massacre which Bashar al-Assad has for years inflicted on his people, and which has led to the rise of religious extremism and the emergence of ISIS.

I mention all this by way of example, because I suspect that by telling the story of these two women, I am telling the tale of so many families, living side by side. And what of their heroic sons, who will stand on the front line and open fire against one another? I know that no matter how many times this moment is written about it will never be enough to let you, the distant reader, truly feel what it means to point a gun at your supposed enemy, and how your heart sinks when the trigger is pulled—remembering that these are the sons of two neighbours. And thus, in this tense moment in a battle scene in the countryside outside Damascus, there lurks a backstory. And for you, the reader, whether you are from the West, whether you're an Arab or wherever you're from, a scene like this might touch the depths of your heart, it might hurt you and trouble you, quite simply because it takes us to the essence of humanity.

Time and again, this is one of the major moral dilemmas of life and death.

How could we forget, for example, a classic like *Les Misérables*? Victor Hugo's historical novel did more to immortalize the ideals and symbols of the French Revolution than all the rhetoric and tomes of research that have dealt with the topic. A character like Gavroche Thénardier, a young boy who died in the 1832 uprising, makes more of an impression on us than any number of political slogans; he is a vivid historical personality who will never die. A character like this makes us feel we share in his history, in his personal tragedy, and this is the magic of literature: that deep human sense of belonging, of empathy, that displaces our own national and religious loyalty and encourages us to identify instead with the idea of free humanity.

The issue here is not whether we can prove that literature is something which rallies mankind towards a more beautiful and noble world; at first glance this seems self-evident and banal, a derivative mantra that is often repeated by writers the world over. The problem is not what writers have to say to each other about it; the problem is with the writers themselves. They—and many authors are indeed aware of this—constitute an outer frame which binds society together at the edges, keeping it balanced and complete. But when we talk about art and literature and whether they are universal and indivisible, what we really need to talk about is how we can transform these ideals into reality and what tools we have at our disposal to achieve it.

The problem really lies in providing access to literature, especially in poor countries scarred by wars and revolutions, where what they really need is channels through which they can access the works of their literati. The issue is complex, and I find considerable inequity in the interplay between certain writers, translators and major publishers, including those of literature produced in the Arab world. For example, very little is known about the Syrian novel, despite the attention paid to Arab culture by translators and orientalists. We didn't see any serious interest in what Syrian writers were producing until the beginnings of the revolution in 2011, although since then this interest has grown as the tragic conflict and humanitarian disaster has escalated, and with the emergence of the religious monstrosity ISIS and the Islamist jihadi battalions—a terrifying and yet alluring subject matter for the West. Attention is therefore focused on what we write from a political perspective, but there isn't the same interest in getting to know us or our culture, or shining a spotlight on the writers of this country. The literary domain is dominated by politics and sensational topics which get the media excited. This is something we should stop and consider, and not ignore. I feel we should be able to engage in a dialogue based on curiosity about seeing us as we really are and getting to grips with this frightening world we belong to.

It would seem, however, that the mechanism responsible for turning literature into a universal language, a process where cultural institutions play the dominant role, is in itself flawed, simply because publishers are limited in their knowledge of the "other" world. This ignorance stems from the prevailing assumption that the Arab world, for example, is the weaker party, with its dictatorships and lack of freedom of speech, where written works are confiscated and writers and activists arrested. This assessment is made using the West as the yardstick, with all its cultural institutions and organizations promoting the rule of law, education and development. But it isn't fair to compare the literary worlds of two regions without looking closely at the differences in terms of culture, the level of socio-economic development and the very distinct forms of government. This is the responsibility that lies squarely on the shoulders of Western publishing houses and cultural institutions, as well as the editors and translators who move between these two worlds.

The difficulty also stems from the tendency, often if not always, to assume a position of superiority, especially given the chaos in the Middle East and the spread of the radical Islamist jihadi fighters—the unintended outcome of the Arab revolutions—all of which has made it clear that the Arab populations have just two options to choose from: either brutal dictatorships or barbaric religious extremism. So how can I, for example, talk about art and literature as a universal language if I am governed by a predetermined set of off-the-shelf templates and stereotypes about me and my literature? This is a legitimate question, because it is exactly what is happening, and yet, on the other hand, we have to recognize the considerable effort made by the many institutions and translators and writers worldwide—in spite of these concerns being marginal in a consumer-driven industry—who are trying to discard the clichés and to present us as we really are, to humanize us. It's fair to say there is a long and major struggle ahead—not to make literature a universal language and a route to dialogue and knowledge, because it already is that—but to create access by opening up channels that might bring literature to readers around the world.

As a Syrian writer, to me it is essential that there are workshops and forums for dialogue between Syrian writers and writers from around the world, about literature and its role in the stillborn process of democratic change in Syria, and about the perception of the "other". It is important that this dialogue is built on an awareness of and familiarity with the literature of these writers who are still so little known. So when we start discussing the importance of art and literature as a common human language capable of launching us into a brave new world, a more just and better-informed one, I think it's important first to learn the alphabet of this common language that is the literature and art of the "other", or else we will find ourselves echoing what has already been said time and time again—empty statements about the role of art in effecting change, the priorities in writing and the link between aesthetics and the ability to change reality— without these theories actually having any true impact.

Literature is our parallel life, the place where history becomes immortal. By bearing witness to our ugliness and our beauty alike, literature opens up the secrets of human brutality. It gives us our heroes and it is our eyes which yearn to humanize this savagery, to make sense of it and to turn it on its head. Literature is that eye which stares unflinchingly into your eyes and becomes a part of your life. With the breadth and depth of knowledge we gain from literature, we are more able to identify with that "other" which we formerly did not understand. And thus literature has so much potential: it can throw wide open the door of hope, it can pull up the roots of hatred and racism, and it can bring the light of vision and insight into this blind world.

Translated by Ruth Ahmedzai Kemp

WHEN IDEAS
FALL IN LINE

ASMAA AL-GHUL

I N EARLY APRIL 2015, journalist Razan Madhoon posted a picture of herself on Facebook, sparking a tirade of criticism and igniting a larger controversy. There were nearly two hundred comments beneath Razan's photograph, most reprimanding her for abandoning correct Islamic attire and taking off the veil. Everyone agreed that what she did was wrong and tantamount to abandoning religion—and everyone considered it a public issue, not a personal matter.

Has living under blockade in the Gaza Strip for nine years brought us to a point where people's ideas are so similar, and those who agree with Razan's decision are so rare? To the point where the same women who seem open-minded when they see us unveiled in public then respond to a photograph with such anger and bigotry?

Razan's decision challenged people in a way she did not intend. It stirred fears of change, fears of lifting the blockade... *for what would happen if our women acted as she did*, they wonder? Razan gave voice to a question that has remained unspoken for years in a climate where individual freedoms and choices are lacking, replaced instead with the ruthless will of the masses. When it comes to the most basic women's issues, the Strip is governed by family values and ideas of honour and shame.

This is what the blockade does to the Gaza Strip: it imprisons the mind. The blockade is not about making people starve; it is about whether they can travel and immerse themselves in new experiences, enabling them to breathe new life into their thoughts and understand that as humans, we are changeable beings; we shift and might believe today what we opposed yesterday.

The current situation in Gaza is not about opposing an openness to the world, it is about fighting the idea of it, and the deep fears that openness provokes. Religious conservatives consider a woman removing her veil so publicly, and with such audacity, to be an affront to their own identity, having convinced the public that they themselves are "angels" with a monopoly on religion. It challenges the righteousness of those who say they can do no wrong as long as they practise their faith fervently and piously. Both the blockade and Gaza's conservative nature have enabled this, as have three wars in six years, erasing people's memories of happiness and bringing them face to face with death.

Hamas emerged and took advantage of this atmosphere—which had, to a certain degree, contributed to its rise—using religion to convince people it could do no wrong. Hamas bans novels like Alaa al-Aswany's *Chicago* and censors films at festivals, vetting them with a committee composed of its own members; and this, when there are no cinemas in Gaza to begin with. They see books, art and the spread of reading as a key threat to their existence as a movement, because thanks to these things, people will soon discover how empty much of their religious and political rhetoric truly is.

This is precisely what happened to Razan Madhoon and her husband—they had been close to partisan Islamist circles, and then they began to read the books they collected while setting up an online book marketplace. They gained a new understanding of life and took a step towards change, one that shocked the majority. For a community of like-minded people, all falling in line, it was a shock that one of their own would step forward and say, "Books changed me. I discovered my mind was under blockade. I decided to stop leading a double life, and to change the way I look to fit what I believe."

Amidst the conservatism encircling the Gaza Strip and the minds of its people, people often bring up the Internet and social media as liberating, but if this has changed their beliefs, it has done so only slightly. Here, social media is a mirror, a means of reflecting social reality. Gunshots and marching gunmen drown out words in this reality; art and literature can scarcely be heard. Here, reality binds the sanctity of religion to the sanctity of resistance and the liberation of land.

Art, literature and cinema are beyond the comprehension of governments that use religion to control entire societies, and that reject art and deal with it only when it suits their ideologies. They print books of poetry with no mention of the divine, the self, or love; they stage plays about the resistance with no women actors, distorting art itself to make it fit with their vision of the world.

I remember arguing with a representative from the Ministry of Culture in Gaza when the government was in the hands of Hamas. I knew the novel *Chicago* was banned because it contains a single scene of a woman masturbating, in allusive language. "Relationships are part of society," I told him, "so how can you ban novels because they contain sex scenes?" In response, the ministry representative told me: "The perverse are drawn to perversion"—by which, of course, he meant me!

The easiest way to silence someone here is to criticize their honour and morals, and this will remain so as long as the religious ideal entails a set of checkboxes: the length of your beard, how diligently you attend mosque, and how loose and modest your clothing is. I am shocked by how widespread the trappings of religiosity are. Those who call for religious practices to be universally followed, and those who give little weight to individual decisions and free will in religion are equally pervasive—even though the Koran urges us to use our minds and think for ourselves in more than thirty verses.

Same clothing, same thoughts, same words... this is what governments with dogmatic ideologies strive for: like-minded thoughts, and for the people thinking them to become identical copies of one another.

Shortly after this controversy erupted, I wrote an article about Razan, which was published in *al-Monitor* in English translation. At the time, I did not think about targeting a specific audience, attracting Western readers, or the fact that it was published in English. I never would have thought the article exoticizing or orientalist... I simply thought this was an important issue that deserved to be covered.

I have no agenda for what I should or should not write, and I do not think we should refrain from focusing on women's clothing in Gaza because it is a subject of interest for the West, or a means of Western voyeurism of the East. I believe any idea is fit to be written about, on any platform and in any language, so long as it is not dictated by ideology.

But life under occupation makes speaking freely a difficult task. When you say "individual freedom", you find yourself following it with the phrase "your freedom ends where others' freedom begins". When you talk about writing and expression, you find yourself speaking about red lines and what will not offend religion or insult the resistance. When you talk about human rights, they say "this is the time for liberating the land from occupation, not liberating women", and though you respond swiftly, with "we cannot liberate the land without also liberating the people", this has become a cliché, albeit true. Under occupation, you are never allowed to be free with your ideas, writing or thoughts—you must always rein them in, and learn to speak softly.

What ignited the public's outrage was not only that Razan had taken off the veil, but that she continued to speak to the press about it as if it were a perfectly normal act. They saw her decision as something to be ashamed of, and airing it in public even more so. They were further angered that instead of sweeping the issue under the rug, I upheld my role as a journalist and refused to cast it aside.

It did not occur to any of the activists berating me that this was just an article, and that I have a right to discuss social issues. Here in the Gaza Strip, where we live in a virtual factory of news, how can we not sanctify journalism and uphold its importance? Yet forbidden topics such as the veil can be traced back to the old triad of taboos in the Arab world: sex, politics and religion.

On the same day the article was published, a student at Birzeit University was openly attacked for posting on Facebook that late President Yasser Arafat was not a martyr. She was bombarded with insults, and the matter culminated in the oppressive Palestinian National

Authority arresting her uncle in Ramallah, and her being threatened with expulsion from university. We are the ones who fashion our own idols.

In the age of the prophets, idols were physical, and easy to break, but in this day and age, idols take the form of ideas, and to smash them or create something else to pray to is difficult indeed.

When the article was published, I was attacked from both sides—Islamists claimed I was calling on women to remove the veil, while leftists accused me of indulging the white colonizer by writing about women, their right to choose their attire, and other topics that please the West. Isn't choosing certain issues over others tantamount to self-censorship? Where is the line between discussing societal issues and pleasing the West and the colonizer? If women, freedom and religion are all issues that pander to the West's interests, should we stop discussing them because we are the victims, with evidently a greater imperialist-colonialist complex than the colonizers themselves? These critics would seem to claim that some articles gratify the colonizer, while others have the potential to liberate us from them.

Yet isn't this line of reasoning just an effect of internalizing the occupation, a symptom of our "Third World" complex, or an attempt to please the "First World"? Isn't engaging with others more important than being divided by race, ethnicity and religion? If we feel we cannot share all aspects of our experience without launching into a diatribe that, in the end, strips us of our humanity, is that too not rooted in a sense of oppression?

How does a young singer like Mohammad Assaf emerge from the blockade, war and hellfire of Gaza to become the first "Arab Idol"? He practised singing all the classic Arabic songs, performing them flawlessly while under blockade in Gaza, and arrived on the world stage with our heritage, giving the world something more than the images of death and destruction that Gaza is known for.

Whenever I participate in conferences or write articles, there is always someone shouting: "Asmaa, talk about the occupation," and so I hastily add a line explaining the occupation. Perhaps people are only accustomed to us presenting ourselves through the occupation; perhaps we are only known through occupation.

Our every experience here in Palestine is intertwined with the occupation. Martyrs, intifada and war live in our memories, but must I intentionally use the occupation to forge my identity and crudely affix it to my art, articles and experiences, as long as it remains ever-present in every story? Is it important to gain sympathy? How important is gaining sympathy if I do not gain reason, truth and influence? Are our authors influential and our artists esteemed simply out of sympathy? Will sympathy liberate our homeland?

Israelis responded to my articles during the 2014 war with vitriol. They accused me of inventing things, going so far as to say I was as skilled as George Orwell at making up stories (which, by the way, I considered a compliment) and that they hoped to see me lying in a grave among the dead. This was not because I wrote about the occupation, but because I wrote of old truths: those of good and evil.

I lost nine family members on 3rd August 2014, in an Israeli bombing that struck my grandfather's home in the Rafah refugee camp, where I was born and raised. It destroyed the house and killed them all. When I reported this, most comments were from Israelis or Israeli sympathizers, brazenly calling me a liar.

I figure that, like us, they have one storyline, one tune to sing along to, even though Israel is not under blockade like the Gaza Strip. What else could explain the lack of diversity, the failure to believe others? Ideology, once again. An open society like Israel too can fall under the blockade of an ideology it creates for itself, one about its right to the land, one that says we Palestinians are intruders. They believe it and hand it down from one person to the next, and when I tell the story of how my family died, how they put the bodies of the children in the ice-cream-shop freezer because the hospital freezers were full, they call me a liar.

How do others' worldviews develop, how do ideas become words that make their way into the world? Each thought is determined by others. Each thought leaves its mark on millions of minds. I cannot justify or attack them, yet nor can I remain silent. There will come a point when we understand the difference between the silence of respect for others' opinions, and the silence of weakness. In society today, we need to learn to apologize when we are wrong, and to thank others when they have taught us something.

I spent days penning a response to my critics, discussing their crude contradictions. They accuse us of providing the West with what it desires, while here we suffer, oppressed. Meanwhile there are living examples of orientalism in free countries: those who offer their nations as the end goal of humanitarian or political asylum; the city upon a hill, the holy grail for the rest of the world.

So let me thank you for sparking these thoughts, and providing the kindling for this article.

Translated by Elisabeth Jaquette

LITERATURE:
FORBIDDEN, DEFIED

MAHMOUD DOWLATABADI

W HEN I AM EXPECTED to write about literature
nowadays, regrettably, the first thing that crosses
my mind are obstacles to literature, roadblocks on its
path to being created; as if someone is whispering to
me: "Those days are gone, those good and glorious
days!" suggesting through this Persian saying that the
best period for creating serious works of literature is in
the past. Though in art every innovation and creation,
every novelty in style or unexpected development is the
product of a process that turns the impossible into new
possibilities, and through the impossible creates conditions that stimulate rather than stifle the creative spirit
or thwart this most humanely peaceful act. My essay
however will allude to the fact that there are actions
that ultimately forbid creativity, in its widest sense, as
practised everywhere.

This preamble suggests to the reader the eternal and
ever-present problem of censorship, a stumbling block
to creativity that seems to be the prerogative of states
and political regimes. Yet this represents only one aspect
of the problem. The cultural history of the twentieth
century demonstrates that rulers and their mercilessly

sharp tools—including incarceration and torture—were not a match for the writer's pen. We know that when writers were able to survive, they triumphed over dark and oppressive conditions, and literary works were produced, published and propagated. And if they were unable to write in their native countries, they crossed borders, remaking themselves in the process. And thus it always was that the literary genum overcame all kinds of obstacles placed before it by practitioners of power, and authors succeeded in fulfilling the mission of reporting history to the world. But, in my view, the impediments to the creation of literature nowadays are larger and more pervasive than overt censorship and its enforcement.

To me, denying and defying the creation of literature appears to be, in this age of new technology, a universal phenomenon, one rooted in disturbing the relations that govern literature's universal sense, disrupting all the relations and distorting all the norms that once governed its creation. New relations and personages begin to rear their heads, shadowy faces in twilight environs, but fairly fixed relations are forged or uncovered, and new creatures begin to show themselves. Many prominent writers talk about the disruptive role played by computers in the process of reading, and they denounce certain aspects of these developments, believing that they tend to hinder readers' relationship with books. In our country, this medium, seemingly a miracle of humanity, is criticized and brought under control, mostly for ethical reasons. In my view, however, this miraculous herald of new potentialities ought to be examined from other angles as well, most significantly from the point of view of anarchy of expression and the domination of many superficial values over its devotees, together with the expansion of a kind of information that is expository rather than thought-provoking. This phenomenon, placed in the service of easy entertainment, appealing to child and adult alike, always features news that astounds, spiced with images that may be concocted or genuine. In whatever guise, the information must, however, be presented in an entertaining way to be able to produce a momentary thrill.

I have personally deprived myself of this blessing, a fact that compounds my ignorance in this area. Yet I refuse to convert, because I believe that these miraculous devices are designed either for the entertainment of the masses or for killing time. The truth is, though, that estrangement from popular culture is hard to bear as well, resembling the act of being sober in the presence of merry-making drinkers. I am told that now everyone can have his or her own podium and microphone, publishing house and filmmaking studio, and much more, and that now every single individual can express an opinion on every issue—and this, I think, is the most populist aspect of this fantastic technology without which contemporary life would be crippled.

Besides killing time, wasting lives and offering entertainment of the type that I refer to as "sliding on ice", there is a second issue challenging the creation of literature, and it has had much practical significance to me, so I wish to address it here briefly. While the previous issue was that of "hindering" literature, this phenomenon I call "defying literature". If my previous remarks related to censorship and its enforcement, to time-wasting easy entertainment or to possibilities of self-expression that resemble tabloid journalism, it is also a problem that the teachings and pronouncements of official media hardly ever encourage or tolerate any literature outside of their own, and the book market is affected similarly. Oscar Wilde is supposed to have once said something to the effect that, in the past, books were written by the literati and read by the masses; now they are written by the rabble and read by nobody! Could Wilde have imagined that the day would come when, in addition to all that, poets and writers would not only have their own websites, but would write and self-publish, instantaneously?

Now imagine all that in the context of this loose talk about "the death of the author" on the tip of every wagging tongue! Over the past thirty-odd years, I have personally not heard any news about any literary work of some weight or worth being displayed in the windows of bookstores in my city, in my country. And if there are some, there's hardly ever a reader to purchase it. "You know," a friend was telling me recently, "it is hard to read books"! After all, in our chaos-ridden cities, where ill-fated people are running aimlessly, concerned about their stagnating incomes and sky-rocketing expenses, how much time does one have left in the day to look for a book, find it, purchase it, and read it too?

Yes, in its deepest sense, defying literature is an all-inclusive tendency that has crept up on us unnoticed, and I, for one, have not heard of anybody or any group facing up to it and questioning it. Clearly, no writer is prepared to own up to the fact that he or she has been defeated, and admit that "the calamity and catastrophe of history has paralysed me". Because of this, the widespread phe-nomenon of "defying literature" is profoundly political too, and I suppose that such a reality was revealed once in aspects of Beckett's and Camus's writings and a little earlier in Kafka's works. Reactions to the two world wars and a profound understanding of the violence of modern crimes with all their appalling ramifications and attempts against humanity by and at the hands of humans gave us experience of such terrifying dimensions, far too awe-inspiring to allow the possibility of analysing and recog-nizing its banal logic. This means that, at least in view of the social elite, understanding and comprehension were defied. As such, the production both of literature and of its contemplative and historical criticism continued, making it possible for us, now a curious and secluded bunch, to hold up signs showing the nature and extent of war's devastations, even though there was no clear perspective before us. The Cold War was raging and Vietnam continued to burn in a hellish fire.

And before we were to bid goodbye to the century there appeared a new kind of literature, at once colour-ful and cunning: the life narrative of peoples trying to free themselves of the shackles placed on their souls by what was left of colonialism, of multinational companies producing bananas, sugar cane and minerals; a literature at once native and regional, at once severe and seductive and sparkling, truly magical. And thus it was that a litera-ture deeply rooted in life and circumstance, and featuring characters previously unknown in literature, continued to live and breathe, holding before us a variegated canvas of corners of our world that we did not know about, the secret of its popularity being the presence of lively and dynamic characters flowing on the riverbed of social life in every clime.

This was character creation of the kind that Virginia Woolf referred to when she said that after Dostoyevsky there remains no place for creating characters. This would be like Dostoyevsky claiming that after Shakespeare there remains no place for creating characters, something which he did not say. I am not sure, but I venture to say that Woolf's words marked the demise of character creation, when many works began with the author's words and ended with the life of the author. Eliminating character from works of literature has its own causes and consequences, of course; what is certain is that getting rid of characters would be tantamount to getting rid of the author himself. Our author Sadeq Hedayat had grasped this point when he said that if you have characters you have a story; otherwise you do not. He might have continued as well, saying, I imagine, that otherwise you are a writer of life narratives, maybe even your own life narrative, but you are not a story-writer.

I cannot tell what the situation is in the West; all I know is that as seasoned a teacher of literature as Harold Bloom, in his book on the lives of one hundred writers, expresses his displeasure at the absence of genius in literature, and its giving way to a kind of levelling. According to him Shakespeare is the Western world's main benchmark in something that is now under duress; Goethe represents the breath of Western literary culture, a culture whose fabric has been torn asunder by a universal network of information and media entertainments, by undue and unnecessary deviations and diversions, by pseudo-literacy and education through computer networks that are the enemy of deep reading. From this vantage point, Bloom says that just at the point where our high culture is approaching its end, enmity with genius appears to be so rampant as to approach some sort of mass ideology.

I neither reject what I have cited from Bloom, nor endorse it. Suffice it to say that it has been a long time since I came across the likes of Albert Camus and Heinrich Böll. And I know nothing about Asian literature, except for the brilliant work by the Japanese writer Yasunari Kawabata which has been translated into Persian as *The House of Sleeping Angels*. How about my own country, Iran? Here, amid the ups and downs and pitfalls of our modern history, the situation has unfolded differently. As a modern phenomenon, Iran's literature began at the threshold of the Constitutional Movement—that is about a century ago. Unfortunately, our contemporary history is a story of successive *coups d'état*: from the Constitution to Reza Shah's coup to his abdication; Mohammad-Reza Shah's accession, followed by the coup of 1953; and then the Islamic Revolution.

As you see, we must regrettably use military landmarks for the purposes of literary periodization. The era that relates to our discussion here is the mature literature that began to blossom after the 1953 coup. In a sense, that political setback became an impetus for our intellectual community to turn its gaze towards literature, mostly through translations of the literary masterpieces of the world, but also and along with it, through the writing of poems and plays and stories and novels; and simultaneously through delving into the classical literature of the Persian language, which is unique. It should not come as a surprise then to say that in a relatively short time, with the works of poets Farrokhzad, Shamlu and Sepehri, playwrights Radi, Beyzai and Saedi, and fiction writers Golestan, Golshiri and Mahmud, a kind of renaissance occurred in the modern literature of Iran. In the end, the late Shah's security apparatus could not tolerate the social and political implications of this literature, and many writers suffered indignity, insult and incarceration.

Before long the Islamic Revolution took place, and shortly afterwards war was inflicted on our country, a war which both the people and the army fought heroically. Many lives were sacrificed and untold assets were destroyed. Huge emigration and massive purges depleted the ranks of the country's intellectuals and writers. The social fabric unravelled and, as society was reorganized, several writers and poets were murdered. Once I had a chance to look back I saw a thirty-odd-year period of immobility and stasis, which I lamented deeply. Every revolution makes its own writers and poets from the ranks of those who are willing to toe the line of a particular ideology. However, in this case, many of the writers who stayed behind in Iran were products of an orientation towards the West or the Soviet Union, and they could not write in such a way as to satisfy the demands of the new Islamic regime, so they too were caught up in the web of censorship, self-censorship and all that entailed, an adjustment that was far from easy.

That situation resulted in an irremediable rupture in a literary tradition that had been looking to the future for over a century. And this happened at a time in our culture when we were told that that there was no future, that we were all living out the tail end of history. This assertion could be heard in our country as well; we were witnessing it on our television screens. First came that most horrific of destructions in New York, then the shock-and-awe show in Baghdad, which radiated upon us the most brilliant evil in history. And we thought we had survived a revolution and eight years of war! What vain thoughts those were! The fire that had been ignited in the Middle East had no intention of abating, far from it. Recently, the United Nations has issued a proclamation stating that—possibly!—genocide may have occurred in Iraq.

Yes, that indeed is our story; and through that story I have come to comprehend something that I am calling "literature defied". What would you do if you were in my place? There I was, fascinated by the literature of the world, by literature in my own country. And I thought of humanity as being distinguished by its dignity and nobility. The truth, however, is that I now ask myself every minute: why write at all? How can my work or that of people like me anywhere in the world have any impact on human crime? In our quest of many years in the depth of our solitary souls, have my fellow writers and I been utterly routed by the shameless pain that has been inflicted on us and that has given itself the mighty name of history? Are we being asked to accept that we have reached the end of all human values in literature? Is all the ugliness and disorder that we are witnessing now part of the same pattern of life that used to lead humans forward, or rather that humanity used to lead forward?

Yes, I want to say that if inside the cocoon of our solitude we, the writers of the world, have been overwhelmed by the enormity of history's shamelessness, if we have reached the end of everything good and wholesome in literature, it is because of the ravages of the same unseemly force to which we have no choice but to give the name of "history". And yet, I begin to argue with myself and conclude in the end that what we are witnessing now may well be the last march of dying postcolonial dictatorships that have resulted in the eruption of savagery long dormant underground. And I recall that the god of death in Mesopotamian mythology, which once lived under the earth, may now be rearing its head one last time.

All my work and all my life have been devoted to observing and listening to and honing and recording the "human" creature, and now I see what humans are doing to humans: the ferocity, the viciousness! Yet, friends, wherever we are or will be, in whatever language we have written, are writing, or will go on writing, let us consider this serious question: have our insights and our values not been defeated by a world whose practical logic we do not know? Has what we have recorded in praise of knowing and doing not suffered a setback caused by the forces of ignorance, a combination of force and ignorance? The realization of the insufficiency of our intelligence may well lie in acknowledging this rupture. And this is the one step forward that we can take in the direction of empathy and friendship; that is, if there is still time left to take this one last step. And so it is that we can move forward.

Translated by Ahmad Karimi-Hakkak

"LOVE" AND "OBLIVION"

HANNA KRALL

"Żal" is the title that arches over this collection of four separate books by Polish author Hanna Krall. The word is difficult to translate: a mix of melancholy and bittersweet nostalgia that permeates story after story of people whose lives were formed—or deformed—by the Holocaust. Survivors, children of survivors. Their protectors. And children without parents searching for their past... Now spread all over the world.

"My work as a journalist," writes Krall, "taught me that stories that are completely logical and clear, without mysteries or missing parts, are often untrue. And that things for which there is no explanation really do happen."

In probing the overlap between the inexplicable and the real, Hanna Krall creates a prose that borrows as much from authorial imagination as from journalistic technique. And in so doing brings us closer to the people whose lives she saves from oblivion by sharing them with us.

(Philip Boehm, translator)

LOVE

From *Tam już nie ma żadnej rzeki*
(*No River Runs There*)

—— I ——

"**N**OW I'D LIKE to hear a story from you," I said.
(I always end readings by asking the audience
that. "Tell me a story. A true one… Something important… About yourself or someone else…")

I switched off the microphone.

Then there was silence, as people wondered whether
they knew a story that was important. And whether they
wanted to entrust it to me.

When they do have something to share they're usually
a little embarrassed, and their words are a little disjointed.

The woman who approached me in Gothenburg had nearsighted grey eyes. Her words were carefully chosen:

"Alicja, the Polish maid, loved Meir, my uncle. She saved him. She died of longing for him. My uncle looked like Rudolph Valentino."

She handed me a calling card: "Helen Zonenshein, Professor of Philosophy." She smiled restrainedly, in Scandinavian fashion.

"I've carried her inside me all my life, this Polish maid Alicja."

— 2 —

Rudolph Valentino?

The photographs showed a rather ordinary-looking man.

"Look at his eyes…" the professor suggested. "You see, they're like almonds. And his gestures. And his slender figure… Anyway you recognized him right away."

He wasn't hard to recognize.

He used to bow. Kneel. Dance a pas de deux. And those seductive smiles, always gallivanting around, dressing up…

Did he annoy people? What do you mean? Everyone

was delighted with him. They loved him. The whole world adored Uncle Meir, perhaps with the exception of the men who did business with him. When it came to doing business he behaved exactly as he did in the drawing room. He was utterly charming, failed to keep his word and didn't remember his promises.

"Meir," his brothers begged him, "be more serious."

They were serious people, those Zonenszajn brothers. Sons of a rabbi from Radom, who yearned to combine Polish Hassidism with Immanuel Kant, in an effort to wed *Modernity* with *Tradition*. But Radom didn't recognize *Modernity*. So Radom told the rabbi his services were no longer needed and the family moved to Warsaw. There they went into business, retail and wholesale: flour, grain, herring, rice. "Dynamic importers of Scandinavian herring"—was what the papers wrote about the firm "Zonenszajn Bros".

So David, the one who bought and sold flour, and the father of six children said:

"Meir, when are you going to grow up?"

Icchak, the one in charge of grain and father of four children, said:

"Meir, when are you…"

Szlomo, who dealt with rice, father of two, said:
"Meir…"

And Aron, who was the youngest in the family, the father of one daughter—the future professor of philosophy—Aron who was slight of build and a little dull, Aron who handled herring and fish products, said:

"Meir!"

They were serious and very mature, those brothers. Still, when Aron stepped into the drawing room no one felt the merrier because Aron had arrived; in fact no one knew for sure whether he was there or not. But whenever Meir appeared, everyone brightened up and the whole world was a nicer place.

Uncle Meir married a wealthy, plump seamstress with long blond hair and a short neck. They hired a maid. "A girl", as they said back then. The girl came from the country. She had quick eyes, a friendly smile, and an unshapely protruding upper lip.

Alicja, the girl from the country, fell in love with Uncle Meir.

My heavens, everyone fell in love with him, but not for real. No one treated him seriously. No one with the exception of the girl from the country.

—4—

During the war Alicja proved herself brave and capable. She arranged fake documents. She bribed the guard…

Thanks to Alicja they got out of the ghetto—Uncle Meir, his brother Aron and their families.

Meir was the last one out. He was afraid. He hesitated to the end, but then he left the ghetto in style. He donned riding boots and breeches and a jacket cut from a bright chequered blanket—and no sooner was he out than a blackmailer pulled him into the nearest entryway.

"Money!"

Uncle Meir took money out of one boot and handed it over. Then he took money from the other boot—and handed that over as well. The blackmailer counted the bills and stashed them away.

"Now may I go?" Uncle Meir asked, shaking.

"Wait," said the blackmailer.

The man reached into his wallet, counted out some bills and gave Uncle Meir half.

"Here, you have to live too."

The whole world adored Uncle Meir, so why shouldn't a blackmailer love him as well?

"Go and live," the man repeated, patting Uncle Meir on the shoulder.

So Uncle Meir went. And lived.

— 5 —

Alicja found everyone a place on the Aryan side. She brought them food. Arranged for doctors. Once when she was returning from the country with contraband meat they arrested her. She wound up in Auschwitz. There she ran into Uncle Meir's cousin Gienia. "I managed to get hold of a little blue pot with a handle made of wire," Gienia wrote after the war from Jerusalem to her family in Oslo. "When it was still dark, before roll call, I would run to the kitchen. Alicja would take a ladle and scoop up some thick soup from the bottom of the pot, just for me…"

— 6 —

The ones who perished:

David, who bought and sold flour, along with his
    wife and six children,
Icchak, grain, with his wife and four children,
Szlomo, rice, with his wife and two children.

The ones who survived, thanks to Alicja:

Uncle Meir with his wife and daughter,

Aron, Meir's brother, with his wife and daughter
   (the future professor of philosophy),
Gienia, Meir's cousin.

— 7 —

The surviving families met with Alicja in Łódź. They
decided to leave the country.

Before they left they had to do something about Alicja.
They found her a husband. He was OK.

He's pictured in a photo in the family album. Blond
hair, receding chin, honest eyes and a big snub nose.

"He wasn't ugly," said Helen. "He wasn't handsome.
He wasn't dumb. He wasn't smart. He was OK. He kept
his promises and didn't resemble Rudolph Valentino in
the least."

— 8 —

They said:

"This will be best, dear Alicja. You'll have a home,
you'll have children. And God willing you'll all be able
to visit us in Norway someday..."

Alicja listened and understood. She was going to have a home. And children.

"We'll remember you as long as we live, dear Alicja…"

They kept their word. From Oslo they sent money, and from Israel they sent citrus fruit.

"Dear Gienia, I received the dollars…" Alicja wrote on a New Year's card.

"I hereby confirm the receipt…" she wrote on the "internal export" form from the PKO bank.

"God, why is fate so hard on me? Why can't we be together? You write telling me that I should act mature. I'm being mature, so why is it so hard for me? Still, somehow I believe that someday I'll be with you…" wrote Alicja.

"I hereby confirm the receipt…"

"I received the dollars…"

"I'm sorry to send you sad news. My wife is in the psychiatric hospital…" Alicja's husband wrote to Oslo.

—9—

Two subjects were constantly present in Helen's family: Alicja and ladies' stockings.

Stockings were a cheery subject. Aron immediately understood the future of nylons, and Meir brought in the women who owned the boutiques. Aron appreciated the significance of pantyhose, Meir brought in… Aron had the vision. Meir had the charm. The firm "Zonenshein Bros" prospered.

Alicja was a sad subject.

"What about Alicja?" Helen's mother asked, concerned. "Did you get a letter?"

"She's not doing well," Meir's wife would say and sigh out loud.

"Any news from Alicja?" asked Uncle Meir.

"Bad news, very bad," Helen's father would say, sadly, lowering his voice.

"Why don't you invite her?" Helen asked. "She misses you."

"To Oslo?" they asked, puzzled. "What would she do here?"

"Right," said Helen. "She's just a Polish girl from the country. What could a Polish girl from the country possibly do with you in Oslo?"

"Don't shout," Mother pleaded. "We're grateful to her. We're helping her. What more can we do?…"

"When I first became ill I had suicidal tendencies, but now they've passed… Naturally I'm supposed to avoid emotional encounters. My son visits me in the hospital twice a year. When my husband divorced me he became my guardian, but now he doesn't care any more. If you want to, please send either used clothing or lemons and oranges, the import duty isn't too high on those…" wrote Alicja.

The last letter from Poland was written by her former husband:

"I'm sorry to send you sad news. Alicja has passed on."

Helen Zonenshein ran away from home.

She became a waitress, found work as a nanny and earned enough for a ticket to the United States. She lived in California, with other young Jews who had run away from home.

— I O —

They went without shoes. They wore flowers in their hair. They repeated *I love you* and talked about their bourgeois families that they hated.

Helen told the story of Alicja.

"For them she remained a Polish girl from the country. She managed to get them out to the Aryan side, but in their eyes she was never anything but a Polish girl from the country…"

"What kind of side?" asked the young American Jews.

The young American Jews who were being looked after by Rabbi Shlomo Carlebach.

Reb Shlomo played the guitar and told stories about the tzadiks who were his masters. These masters lived one or two hundred years ago, and the towns where they taught had exotic names: Izbica, Turzysk, Gostynin, Kotzk...

"Tzadik Mordechai Yosef of Izbica taught us: whenever you truly love, your love will summon him from the earthly world and from the heavenly one..." said Shlomo Carlebach, and Helen thought about Alicja's love.

Shlomo Carlebach also told them about tzadik Jehiel Meir of Gostynin, who loaned his tallith to an unknown Jew. When the stranger returned the shawl it was wet with tears. Don't worry, he said, it will dry by tomorrow. I don't want it to dry, Jehiel cried out. I don't ever want it to be dry again! Pack your things, said the stranger. Menachem Mendel of Kotzk is waiting for you. They went together and Jehiel became the student of the famous Kotzker Rebbe. Helen listened to Shlomo Carlebach's story, and thought about Alicja's tears.

Abraham of Turzysk didn't sleep and didn't eat. When asked for the reason, he explained:

"When I was nine years old, my father Mordechai, the tzadik of Chernobyl, woke me at dawn, harnessed the horse and together we climbed into the wagon. We rode out into the forest and came to a clearing where I saw a hut. 'Hold the reins,' said my father. He went into the hut and came back out with a young man. The young man's sad face radiated light. He carefully listened to my father's words. 'Are you sure that's what you have to tell me?' he asked. My father replied: 'I'm sure,' and both men burst into tears. They stood there embracing each other and didn't stop sobbing. Finally they said goodbye and my father climbed onto the wagon. We set off without looking back. When we spotted our home in the distance, I asked: 'Father, who was that person?' 'The Messiah. That was the Messiah, the son of David.' 'What did he want from us?' 'He asked if it was time for him, if he could arrive. I had to tell him the terrible truth: no one is waiting for him yet.'"

"Now would you be able to sleep or eat if you saw the Messiah and if you had learned he wasn't coming to us because no one was waiting for him?" asked Rabbi Carlebach on behalf of Abraham of Turzysk.

But Helen thought about her family. What did the Messiah matter, since they didn't even wait for Alicja.

Carlebach spoke wisely and he sang beautifully, but Helen didn't want to listen to ecstatic songs. She wanted to read books, and moved to Berkeley.

She graduated and went on to finish her Ph.D. She became a professor of philosophy. She returned to Oslo.

She saw Uncle Meir in his armchair, after a stroke. He wasn't capricious. He didn't complain. Didn't ask for anything. He sat there with a happy smile, repeating a single word.

"*Hiné... Hiné...*"

Which means in Hebrew:

Look there...

As if he saw something incredibly beautiful.

He died without anyone realizing.

"*Hiné,*" he whispered, closed his eyes and smiled in delight. A few hours later someone noticed:

"Meir is dead."

Someone said:

"A nice death. God really did like Meir."

That was Aron, Helen's father.

His voice had a clear note of envy.

Even God liked Meir.

But who's going to like people who are small, dull, dependable and serious?...

OBLIVION

From *Dowody na istnienie / Proof of Existence*

GOTHENBURG

P EOPLE WHO HAD LEARNED they were really Jewish
wanted to meet others like them. One Sunday after-
noon a month they would gather inside the cramped
cafeteria of the Yiddish theatre. Dressed in their best
clothes, they huddled around the tiny tables drinking
tea brewed in bags, sweating from the stuffy room and
their own emotions. Lacking all knowledge and unable
to remember, they never stopped swapping stories.

Invited guests came to visit. One renowned critic
lectured on the importance of diversity in literature.
Black poets had revolutionized French poetry. The most

interesting contemporary works are being written by a Canadian conceived in Cyprus and a Yoruba from Nigeria educated in England. The critic used beautiful, carefully chosen words. Meanwhile the audience slipped off one by one into the theatre lobby, where a tall blond man was also holding forth. And even though this man's delivery was rushed and chaotic to the point of being incoherent and hard to understand, the listeners managed to piece together his story, about a man named Leon Eidelberg who had been in the Lwów ghetto with his wife and three-year-old daughter. The little girl was killed, and the wife discovered she was a few weeks pregnant. Eidelberg was assigned to a furrier workshop that also had Polish workers. He told them about his daughter's death and his wife's pregnancy, and that he had to do something, because why should his wife bring another child into the world? Just so there could be another death? When one of the female Polish workers repeated Eidelberg's story at home, her mother said: "Tell that Jewish woman she should have her child and bring the baby to us." And the Jewish woman had the baby. And Leon Eidelberg wrapped his two-day-old son in a newspaper and put him in a bread bag and took him to the workshop and gave him to the Polish woman who worked there.

The war ended; Eidelberg survived. He went to the people he had entrusted with his child. He said: My wife was killed, they're all gone, but my son is alive thanks to you, I'll be grateful to you till the end of my days—and he held out his arms to take the boy. To which the grand-mother—because the worker's mother was already calling herself grandmother, she'd had the baby baptized and given him a first and last name, so that Leon Eidelberg's son was officially named Jerzy Lencki—to which the grandmother called out horrified: "What on earth are you thinking! You're in no condition to take that child. You're dirty and full of lice, first go wash yourself and then come back for the child."

And Leon Eidelberg went and washed himself and got rid of the lice, but when he came back there wasn't a trace of the child, the grandmother or the whole Polish family.

He spent several years searching for them and finally left the country. He settled in Canada and started a new family. Towards the end of his life he wrote a letter to the Polish Red Cross, and they informed Jerzy Lencki that Leon Eidelberg from Toronto was looking for him.

"Then what happened?" The people listening to the man in the lobby of the Yiddish theatre still didn't catch on.

"So I went to Toronto."

"And then?"

"And then I met Leon Eidelberg, my father."

"Your father?"

"We had our DNA tested and it was a ninety-nine percent match."

More listeners came by and each one had to be told from the beginning:

"His father found him."

"He found his father."

"He met with his father."

"They had their DNA tested."

"What did you say to your father?"

"What did you call him? Father? Daddy?"

"I called him Dad. 'Dad, I'm a practising Catholic.' Those were the first words I said to him, over the telephone, while I was still in Poland. And he said: 'I don't care what you are. I'm dying of cancer. I'd like to see you before I die…'"

"Father… His father's… To his father's… Together with his father…" The people who had never been found by anyone repeated with envy and joy.

In the words of the ethnic Yoruba writer from Nigeria that the critic was talking about in the theatre cafeteria:

> Upon the hour of sleep, tell these walls
> The human heart may hold
> Only so much despair.

(from 'To the Madmen Over the Wall' by Wole Soyinka)

Translated by Philip Boehm

SEA OF VOICES

ANDREY KURKOV

T HERE'S A SEA OF NOISE inside me. I hear it only when I listen. There is nothing perilous about this sea—it won't capsize me, although I am a seafaring vessel of sorts. I'm always out on the waves, always sailing, and every one of my voyages swells my internal sea, making it richer and more sonorous, adding voices. That's what this internal sea consists of—the voices that live inside me, in my memory, in my life. My internal sea is so rich with sounds that I rarely cover my ears with headphones, preferring not to listen to music—popular or otherwise—when I'm out. I'm happy enough without it. I'm happy, too, that I have never understood some of the voices that live in my internal sea, and now there is no chance that I ever will. They remain a mystery, which in and of itself highlights the value of being able to hear something and understand it. Within my internal sea I can hear the voices of the Ainu of the Kuril Islands, a northern people who lived on the islands of Japan and in what is now the Russian Far East. Their voices—the voices of the very last Kuril Ainu—were recorded by an ethnologist who recognized the tragedy of a dying language. During the 1970s the Soviet Academy of Sciences published a book about the Kuril Ainu, which was accompanied by a vinyl disc containing an audio recording of their voices. I have come to believe that the Soviet ethnologist who made the recording also, in a way, accompanied the last Ainu on his final journey. The last Kuril Ainu passed away in 1946; all that is left of him is his voice, which I carry with me, thinking of him often. I can hear his voice whenever I like—not only within myself, like the sound of my internal sea, but aloud—I still have the record, and the book. The Ainu had no literature, no written language of their own; they had their voices and their songs. In the future scholars and scientists will understand more about the archaeology of sound. One day they will learn how to retrieve and reconstruct the echo of bygone eras. If they don't, then this task will once again fall to us writers.

In the winter of 1990 my wife and I went travelling in the mountains of Dagestan, a country renowned for its linguistic and cultural diversity. The language of international communication in the region at the time was a simplified Russian, frequently lacking in grammar. Every mountain topped with an ancient settlement had its own language, which was considered to be different from the language of the neighbouring mountain—even if they were in fact virtually identical.

That distant December, after a somewhat adventurous journey, my wife and I reached the top of a mountain with two unequal peaks and, accordingly, two distinct

communities within the same settlement: Lower Kubachi
and Upper Kubachi. By tradition, all Kubachi men were
hunters and jewellers. Gold and silver coffee sets made
by local craftsmen could be found as far afield as Paris
and Brussels.

Several kilometres away on the higher peak of a different mountain were the romantic ruins of the ancient
aul [fortified village] of Amuzgi, which according to
local legend was more than three thousand years old. We
hadn't even heard of Amuzgi before arriving in Kubachi,
but our new Kubachi acquaintance—Gadzhi-Musa,
jeweller and hunter—told us all about the *aul* and its
three remaining inhabitants: an elderly couple and an
old woman. We learned that they had their own Amuzgi
language, which Gadzhi-Musa was familiar with because
he had been friends with the elderly couple's son, who
died during his military service in the Soviet army. He
also said that there had never been any vehicular access
to the *aul*, so it had no roads. The only way to get there
was on foot. It was too dangerous to travel even by donkey,
because most of the journey involved walking along a
narrow wooden ledge fixed to the side of the mountain,
with a sheer drop of two hundred metres below it and
a kilometre-high wall of rock above it.

The day after we arrived in Kubachi we decided
to visit Amuzgi. The temperature was about –20 °C,
which was to be expected for the time of year, and

the foothills below were shrouded in mist. Gadzhi-Musa led us out of the village to the path, and we left Upper Kubachi behind. The walk was not particularly daunting because the precipice below was hidden from view by the mist, which came up almost as high as our wooden ledge.

Eventually the wooden ledge became a path hewn out of the rock, and we finally found ourselves standing amongst the stillness of the ancient ruins. At the very top of the mountain I saw the remains of an ancient mosque. Suddenly, to the left of the ruined mosque I noticed a column of smoke, straight as a birch tree. There was no wind, and the smoke appeared to be coming right out of the ground.

Gadzhi-Musa led us towards the column of smoke and a few minutes later we stopped before a dwelling, which was the lowest I had ever seen—practically a *zemlyanka* [dugout]. The roof came up to my chest, and several stone steps led down to the entrance door, which can't have been more than a metre and half high.

"Wait here," said Gadzhi-Musa, and he went down the steps, opened the door and disappeared inside.

The door closed behind him. My wife and I waited outside. We stood rooted to the spot, as though we were subconsciously trying to blend in, to match the stillness of the ancient, bygone world around us. Our stillness made us more acutely aware of the cold.

After a little while our guide emerged from the dwelling and said that the elderly couple didn't want to invite us in. He added that he would try once more and went back inside. A few minutes later sparks burst from the chimney and the smoke turned dark. The occupants had obviously put some brushwood on the fire. That must have been the moment at which Gadzhi-Musa persuaded them to allow us into their home.

Ten minutes later we were sitting with them around a makeshift iron stove, as though it were a table. A continuous wave of hot air struck my knees, warming my legs. On top of the stove stood a ceramic bowl containing pieces of meat. The old man opened a bottle of vodka, handed each of us a teacup and began pouring straight away, talking to Gadzhi-Musa as he did so. Gadzhi-Musa kept nodding his head, but he didn't translate for us.

In order to avoid causing any offence, my wife, who stopped eating meat when she was a student, asked our guide to mention to our host that she was a vegetarian. Gadzhi-Musa began to explain this to the old man. The old woman, sitting to the left of her husband, looked at Liza in astonishment. The old man appeared to ask Gadzhi-Musa a question, which made him laugh.

"He wants to know whether vegetarianism is the same as homosexuality," explained Gadzhi-Musa, once he'd stopped laughing.

On hearing this my wife took the fork that was held out to her, speared a piece of goat meat that had been dried in the cold mountain air and warmed on the stove, and began to chew it diligently.

Her vegetarian principles were forsaken on that occasion because the concept simply did not exist in the Amuzgi language, and therefore it had no place in local culinary traditions.

As we were walking back, stumbling due to the vodka we had drunk and cautiously peering from the wooden ledge down into the precipice, which was visible now the mist had cleared, Gadzhi-Musa patiently answered my questions.

"How can they possibly survive, cut off like that, and without electricity!" he said. "Back in the 1930s the Soviet authorities tried to make everyone leave the mountain for the towns and villages below. The young people went, but the older ones stayed. Then war broke out and many of them died. When these three die, the Amuzgi will no longer exist! The postman will no longer have to visit once a month to deliver their pension money."

"Will the language die too?" I asked.

"Of course! It's virtually dead already. It used to be written in Arabic script, and then it was converted to Cyrillic during the Soviet era. Except they no longer wrote in it by then—it was purely a spoken language. Any language in widespread use was converted to Cyrillic.

In Derbent the Judeo-Tat language* was converted to Cyrillic, and they even published books in it! But in this case there are only three people left. Two, really, because the old woman who lives with the goat doesn't speak at all any more. So yes, the language will die with them."

It is twenty-five years since that conversation took place, since that cold Dagestani winter. Many years later Gadzhi-Musa came to visit us in Kiev. He had come to deliver a silver coffee set he had made for someone—a coffee pot, an engraved tray and a set of little silver cups, gilded inside. I asked him about the old people of the Amuzgi *aul*. "They're all dead," he replied, but he said nothing more about them or the *aul*.

Now the Amuzgi people are somewhere up there, in heaven or wherever they might be, conversing with the Kuril Ainu. Each speaking in their own dead language, yet somehow understanding one another.

While I can hear only music in the dead languages of the Amuzgi people and the Kuril Ainu, another language, which I encountered considerably later, introduced me to new insights and ideas. These insights were given to me in my own language, though when I was first captivated by them at the age of seventeen I gave no thought to the intermediary, to the person who had made them

---

* A language spoken by Iranians who adopted Judaism and fled persecution in the mountains of the North Caucasus.

accessible to me by translating them from Lithuanian into my native Russian.

At the end of the 1970s the Soviet Union was densely populated by a "united" Soviet people, fathered by Lenin and Stalin. Most of these Soviet people were happy with their new identity and collectively contributed to the development of a Soviet economy, Soviet culture and Soviet politics, consciously renouncing their roots. But there were others who continued to acknowledge their ancestors and their country of origin, and quietly, without drawing undue attention to themselves, they did what they could to keep their national cultures alive. One of these "Atlanteans" was the Lithuanian poet Marcelijus Martinaitis, who died in 2013. He spent his life writing Lithuanian ballads in Lithuanian about a Lithuanian hero he had created, by the name of Kukutis.

I don't remember how the Russian translation of *The Ballads of Kukutis* first came into my possession, but I was an instant convert. I became a lifelong devotee of Kukutis, the eternal Lithuanian, in some respects akin to the Wandering Jew; Kukutis, who lost his leg to the First World War but survived it otherwise unscathed; Kukutis, who sees his beloved Lithuania everywhere, even in Paris and Berlin when he and his wooden leg visit these cities on their travels.

In order to get to know Kukutis a little better, I wrote some music to accompany the ballads and made up a few songs of my own about him. In 2004 I happened to hear from some Lithuanian friends of mine that the author of *The Ballads of Kukutis* was alive and still writing ballads about Kukutis. So I called him from Kiev and sang him the songs I had written, based on the Russian translations of his poems. For almost ten years I sang my songs to Marcelijus Martinaitis. During that time I also found out the name of the translator—Grigory Efremov. I learned that Efremov had been friends with Marcelijus Martinaitis his whole life and had been translating his ballads for as long as he'd known him. I tried to visit Marcelijus Martinaitis several times; I would call him whenever I flew to Vilnius. But each time he was either away or too ill to see me. I never got to meet him in person. I did eventually visit his house, though—in June 2014, after he died. His widow invited me into their home, a little wooden house just outside Vilnius, and talked about the life they'd had there together, about her husband's friendship with Grigory Efremov, about the ironic relationship he'd had with many of his Lithuanian colleagues and about many other things too. Back in 2012 I had asked Marcelijus by phone if I could borrow Kukutis for one of my books. "Be my guest," he said. "You can quote the ballads too, if you like!"

So that was how Kukutis ended up in my latest novel. It's a novel about Lithuania and Europe, about the present day and about eternity. I haven't finished writing it yet. Recent events in Ukraine have made it impossible for me to sit down at my desk and complete the final chapters. Recent events in Europe, perhaps I should say? After all, both Lithuania and Ukraine are part of Europe—this ancient, timeless continent that extends beyond wars and epidemics; always at peace, providing work for hundreds of thousands of translators and interpreters, and always in a state of conflict when these translators suddenly vanish, communication breaks down, and different cultures are left regarding one another with mutual suspicion and hostility.

There is still a sea of noise inside me—a sea of words I have heard, words I have spoken in other languages. Amongst the sounds of this sea I can make out a few words in Lithuanian, which is not a dead language—far from it. The language is quite familiar to me these days, thanks to Kukutis and his creator Marcelijus Martinaitis. I already understand several words and phrases. And I rejoice in my understanding, like a child discovering a secret. Every culture, every literature contains a secret. The key to unlocking this secret is the language in which the culture is created, in which its texts are written, in which its ballads are sung and its songs recorded. So many Lithuanian thoughts and ideas were hidden from me behind closed doors, until these doors were opened for me by the translator Grigory Efremov. I hope to meet him one day, to thank him for everything that he has done for Kukutis, for Martinaitis and for me. He brought the three of us together, and in doing so he has enriched my life, made it considerably more interesting. The Kuril Ainu were not so fortunate. There were no translators where they lived—just walruses and seals, wolves and bears. And they are still there today. If the Kuril Ainu had their own Kukutis, whatever he may have been called, he died with them. Leaving no sign that he ever existed.

Translated by Amanda Love Darragh

A RALLYING CRY FOR
COSMOPOLITAN EUROPE

ELIF SHAFAK

WHEN MEHMET CHELEBI, the Ottoman ambassador to France in the eighteenth century, visited the Paris Observatory he was impressed. "They have rendered visible the things that up to this day could only be dreamt of," he commented. "A common man with little knowledge of the stars can now, thanks to these instruments, become a savant." It was this possibility that struck him, the prospect of an ordinary human being surpassing his own limits. If individuals could achieve this transformation, why not nations or entire continents? This, he never said aloud, but perhaps felt deep in his heart, that with the power of knowledge it was possible to alter one's circumstances. If so, Europe must have seemed to him a land where people not only practised the alchemy of turning the invisible into the visible but also dared to change their destiny.

How much of that "European chutzpah and commitment to knowledge" that the Ottoman diplomat had so curiously observed has remained today? While he was moved by the willingness and the capacity to defy boundaries—cultural, geographical, intellectual—it seems today that boundaries are becoming more vital and forceful.

We are in the midst of a newly emerging debate between those who are against and those who are in favour of a common European future. How did we get here?

Until a decade ago there was much optimism that in the increasingly interconnected world, both religiosity and nationalism would lose their appeal for a large number of people, and we would all become gently, almost spontaneously, globalized. This did not happen. At least, not in the way it was predicted.

While new information technologies and mobility of capital have brought us closer than ever before, it hasn't always been "our common humanity" that we've shared and valued. Unfortunately, waves of bigotry, racism, xenophobia and homophobia, too, are in wide circulation across the globe. The Internet does not only distribute democratic, progressive, all-embracing values. It also spreads misinformation, slander and hate speech. Exclusivist nationalisms, far from withering away, have gained ground. Each wave of economic turbulence fans the flames of reactionary narratives. It only takes a perceived crisis to see that underneath the calm and order that we often take for granted, there are old hatreds and animosities, waiting.

In the meantime, the rise of violence, intolerance and misogyny in the Middle East is heartbreaking. We have lost the balance between masculine and feminine energies, a balance that was essential and ancient. On the streets, in the urban squares, in decision-making rooms throughout the region, there are very few women. Masculinity dominates the public space in the Middle East. What we are observing in the region today, however, cannot be isolated from what is happening all around the world. An increase in anxiety, insecurity, conspiracy theories, fear of the Other... Russia is home to a mighty far-right movement. Across South America, India, Pakistan and Turkey, jingoism holds strong. How easy it is for affable neighbours to start hating each other. As human beings we have learned nothing from the mistakes of the past.

All extremist ideologies share one problematic message in common. Whether it is Islamic fundamentalists or the Hungarian far right that wish to produce different ID cards for Gypsies and Jews, they harbour a deep dislike of multiculturalism. Over and over, hardliners preach that we must have a single, monolithic identity. "Are you a Muslim?" they ask. "Be a Muslim. Nothing else! Nothing more!" They tell us it is not possible to be more than one thing at once. "Muslim and secularist and Swedish and European and world citizen and global soul..." for instance. It is ironic that in a world where more and more people dream in more than one language, we are constantly being asked to reduce ourselves to singularity.

One of the most cherished slogans of Turkish ultra-nationalism has been "love it or leave it!" The tone is aggressive, high-handed, unyielding. An anonymous voice orders you to make a choice, once and for all: "If you love your motherland you should not criticize it. If you do criticize, it means you don't love it enough, in which case pack up and go away."

This either/or mentality is at the heart of all kinds of exclusivist ideologies. But the human being, by nature, is a conglomeration of multiple voices. Each and every one of us retains myriad selves. We are never just one single identity.

Perhaps we novelists experience this truth more closely than other people. Our task is to understand human beings in all their complexity. Every writer knows that for a story to exist there must be differences. One cannot construct a story with characters that are exactly the same. And if God is the biggest storyteller, the universe needs diversity to move on.

While ultranationalism thinks in "either/or" terms, cosmopolitanism is the path of pluralism. Ultranationalism loves exclamation marks and full stops! Cosmopolitanism ends each sentence with either a comma or three dots. Rather than reducing human beings to a single label, cosmopolitanism insists on the possibility of multiple allegiances.

But the question remains: who precisely is a cosmopolite? Is it someone who lives in today's major cities such as New York, London or Berlin? Is it someone who has more than one ethnic or racial heritage? Does having a Jamaican father and a Portuguese mother and a Dutch grandmother automatically render one a cosmopolitan? My answer is no; not necessarily. Cosmopolitanism requires not racial hybridity but the *appreciation* of hybridity. It requires consciousness and awareness, not blood and genes.

We have entered the age of global anxiety. Parochialism, nationalism, religious fanaticism and the politics of fear claim to be the only balm to soothe collective worries. Yet all of them are bound to create further divisions and hatred, pushing us further down into a spiral of antagonism. Faced with this tide of extremism, what needs to be done is to swim against it. We must find an embracing, pluralistic narrative that can speak to the minds and hearts of people from different cultural, ethnic and religious backgrounds. A narrative that is not afraid to speak louder than exclusivist voices, whether in Europe or the Middle East or elsewhere. What we need is a compassionate but equally radical and courageous type of humanism. Those of us who happen to come from parts of the world such as Turkey that have lost their multicultural heritage, know that cherishing "uniformity" at the expense of "diversity" and looking for "safety" in "sameness" comes at a sad cost.

WRITERS'
BIOGRAPHIES

ASMAA AL-GHUL, born in 1982, is a Gaza resident writer and journalist, single mother of a boy and a girl. She comes from the Rafah refugee camp on the border with Egypt. Al-Ghul works as Gaza correspondent for *al-Monitor: The Pulse of the Middle East* and at the Lebanon's Samir Kassir Foundation, which campaigns for media freedom.

CHAN KOONCHUNG was born in Shanghai and raised in Hong Kong, where he was a reporter at an English newspaper before he founded the influential *City Magazine*, which he published for twenty-three years. He is a screenwriter and film producer, a co-founder of the environmental group Green Power, a board member of Greenpeace International and a co-founder of an NGO, Minjian International, connecting Chinese intellectuals with their counterparts from Asia and Africa. His first novel, *The Fat Years*, was published in sixteen countries and his second novel, *The Unbearable Dreamworld of Champa the Driver*, has just been published in English. He lives in Beijing.

AMIT CHAUDHURI, the author of five critically acclaimed novels, is a poet, musician and highly regarded critic. He is a Fellow of the Royal Society of Literature and Professor of Contemporary Literature at the University of East Anglia. He has contributed fiction, poetry and reviews to numerous publications including the *Guardian*, the *London Review of Books*, the *Times Literary Supplement*, the *New Yorker* and *Granta*. Chaudhuri lives in Calcutta and Norwich.

MAHMOUD DOWLATABADI, one of the Middle East's leading writers, was born in 1940 in a remote farming region of Iran. He spent his early life as a labourer before arriving in Tehran, where he started acting and writing. In 1974, Dowlatabadi was imprisoned by the Shah's secret police for two years because: "everyone we arrest seems to have copies of your novels, so that makes you provocative to revolutionaries." His books include *Kelidar* (a ten-volume portrait of Iranian village life), *Missing Soluch* and *The Colonel*, shortlisted for the Haus der Kulturen der Welt Berlin International Literature Award, longlisted for the Man Asian Literary Prize, and awarded the 2013 Jan Michalski Prize for Literature.

AYELET GUNDAR-GOSHEN was born in Israel in 1982. She holds an MA in Clinical Psychology from Tel Aviv University, has been news editor on Israel's leading newspaper and has worked for the Israeli civil-rights movement. Her film scripts have won prizes at international festivals including the Berlin Today Award and the New York City Short Film Festival Award. *One Night, Markovitch*, her first novel, won the Sapir Prize for best debut and is published by Pushkin Press; her second novel, *Waking Lions*, will be published by Pushkin Press in 2016.

HANNA KRALL, born in 1935 in Poland, survived the Second World War hiding on the "Aryan" side in Warsaw. Her family perished in the war. She began her writing career as a journalist. Since the early 1980s she has worked as a novelist and reportage writer. She has received numerous awards, such as the underground Solidarity Prize, the Polish PEN Club Prize, the German Würth-Preis and the Austrian Herder Prize. Translated into seventeen languages, her work has gained widespread international recognition. *Chasing the King of Hearts* was shortlisted for the Angelus Central European Literary Award and the UK *Jewish Quarterly-*Wingate Prize.

ANDREY KURKOV was born in St Petersburg in 1961. Having graduated from the Kiev Foreign Languages Institute, he worked for some time as a journalist, did his military service as a prison warder in Odessa, then became a writer of screenplays and author of critically acclaimed and popular novels, including the bestselling *Death and the Penguin*. Kurkov has long been a respected commentator on Ukraine for the world's media, notably in the United Kingdom, France, Germany and the United States.

ALAIN MABANCKOU was born in 1966 in Congo. He is the author of four novels: *African Psycho*, *Broken Glass*, *Black Bazaar* and *Tomorrow I'll Be Twenty* (a fictionalized retelling of Mabanckou's childhood in Congo), and a work of non-fiction, *The Lights of Pointe-Noire*. In 2015, Mabanckou was listed as a finalist for the Man Booker International Prize. He currently teaches literature at UCLA.

ANDRÉS NEUMAN was born in 1977 in Buenos Aires, the son of Argentinian émigré musicians. He grew up and lives in Spain. Included in *Granta*'s "Best of Young Spanish-Language Novelists" issue, he writes novels, short stories, essays and poetry. *Traveller of the Century*, published by Pushkin Press, won the Alfaguara Prize and Spanish National Critics' Prize, and was shortlisted for the *Independent* Foreign Fiction Prize and the International IMPAC Dublin Literary Award. His works have been translated into twenty languages, and Pushkin Press also publishes his novel *Talking to Ourselves* and short-story collection *The Things We Don't Do*.

ELIF SHAFAK is the most widely read female writer in Turkey. Her books include the novels *The Bastard of Istanbul* and *The Forty Rules of Love* and the memoir *Black Milk*. She lives in London and Istanbul.

SAMAR YAZBEK, a Syrian writer and journalist, was born in 1970 in Jableh, near Latakia. A prominent voice supporting human rights and, more specifically, women's rights, Yazbek launched Women Now for Development, an NGO aimed at empowering Syrian women. In 2011 she participated in the uprising against the Assad regime and was forced into exile. For *A Woman in the Crossfire: Diaries of the Syrian Revolution* she was awarded the PEN/ Pinter "International Writer of Courage" Prize, the Swedish Tucholsky Prize, and the Dutch Oxfam/PEN Award. She has lived in Paris since 2013. *The Crossing: My Journey to the Shattered Heart of Syria* was published in 2015 by Penguin Random House.

TRANSLATORS' BIOGRAPHIES

RUTH AHMEDZAI KEMP is a British translator of Arabic, German and Russian, specializing in contemporary fiction, drama and literary non-fiction. She is the translator of *The Bride of Amman*, a novel by Jordanian author Fadi Zaghmout, and the co-translator with Nashwa Gowanlock of *The Crossing* by Samar Yazbek, an account of the Syrian conflict.

PHILIP BOEHM works as a director, playwright and literary translator. He has translated numerous books from German and Polish by authors including Franz Kafka, Hanna Krall and Nobel laureate Herta Müller. Recent awards include prizes from PEN USA and the Polish Institute of Culture, as well as fellowships from the Guggenheim Foundation and the National Endowment for the Arts. He lives in St Louis, where he is the Artistic Director of Upstream Theater.

NICK CAISTOR is a British writer and translator who has translated more than fifty works of fiction from Latin America, Spain and France, as well as publishing works on Mexico City and Buenos Aires and short biographies of Octavio Paz, Che Guevara and Fidel Castro.

ELISABETH JAQUETTE is a translator from Arabic. She holds a BA from Swarthmore College and an MA from Columbia University. Her work has been published in the *Guardian*, *The Book of Gaza* (Comma Press, 2014), *Words Without Borders* and *Asymptote* journal, among other places. She is also the Arabic reading group chair for UK publisher And Other Stories. She is currently translating *The Queue* by Basma Abdel Aziz. The novel is forthcoming with Melville House in 2016.

AHMAD KARIMI-HAKKAK is a professor of Persian Language and Literature at the University of Maryland and author of numerous scholarly monographs, translations and anthologies of Persian literature. His 1995 book, *Recasting Persian Poetry: Scenarios of Poetic Modernity in Iran* has been recognized as a landmark publication all over the world. After a decade of being caught in the web of censorship in Iran, a selection of his numerous Persian-language articles has recently been published as a book under the title of *Bud o Nemud-e Sokhan* (*Literature: Its Existence and Appearance*).

AMANDA LOVE DARRAGH won the 2009 Rossica Translation Prize for her translation of *Iramifications* by

Maria Galina (Glas). She has translated two novels by Andrey Kurkov for Harvill Secker and a number of other novels and short stories by contemporary Russian authors, as well as a diary written during the Siege of Leningrad.

SONDRA SILVERSTON is a native New Yorker who has lived in Israel since 1970. Among her published translations are works by Israeli authors Amos Oz, Etgar Keret, Eshkol Nevo, Savyon Liebrecht and Aharon Megged.

HELEN STEVENSON is a piano teacher, writer and translator, and lives in Somerset. She has translated works by Marie Darrieussecq, Alice Ferney and Catherine Millet, as well as four books by Alain Mabanckou. She is currently working on Mabanckou's most recent novel, *Petit Piment*. Her own recent memoir will be published by Virago in 2016.

ENGLISH PEN

FREEDOM TO **WRITE**
FREEDOM TO **READ**

English PEN's Writers in Translation programme, established in 2005 and supported by Bloomberg and Arts Council England, champions the best literature from around the world. English PEN exists to promote literature and its understanding, uphold writers' freedoms around the world, campaign against the persecution and imprisonment of writers for stating their views, and promote the friendly co-operation of writers and free exchange of ideas.

Each year, a dedicated committee of professionals selects books that are translated into English from a wide variety of foreign languages. We award grants to UK publishers to help translate, promote, market and champion these titles. Our aim is to celebrate books of outstanding literary quality, which have a clear link to the PEN charter and promote free speech and intercultural understanding.

www.englishpen.org

PUSHKIN PRESS

Pushkin Press was founded in 1997, and publishes novels, essays, memoirs, children's books—everything from timeless classics to the urgent and contemporary.

Our books represent exciting, high-quality writing from around the world: we publish some of the twentieth century's most widely acclaimed, brilliant authors such as Stefan Zweig, Marcel Aymé, Antal Szerb, Gaito Gazdanov and Yasushi Inoue, as well as compelling and award-winning contemporary writers, including Andrés Neuman, Edith Pearlman, Erwin Mortier and Ayelet Gundar-Goshen.

Pushkin Press publishes the world's best stories, to be read and read again. Here are just some of the titles from our long and varied list. For more amazing stories, visit www.pushkinpress.com.

=

THE SPECTRE OF ALEXANDER WOLF

GAITO GAZDANOV

'A mesmerising work of literature' Antony Beevor

BINOCULAR VISION

EDITH PEARLMAN

'A genius of the short story' Mark Lawson, *Guardian*

IN THE BEGINNING WAS THE SEA

TOMÁS GONZÁLEZ

'Smoothly intriguing narrative, with its touches of sinister, Patricia Highsmith-like menace' *Irish Times*

BEWARE OF PITY

STEFAN ZWEIG

'Zweig's fictional masterpiece' *Guardian*

TRAVELLER OF THE CENTURY

ANDRÉS NEUMAN

'A beautiful, accomplished novel: as ambitious as it is generous, as moving as it is smart' Juan Gabriel Vásquez, *Guardian*

THE WORLD OF YESTERDAY

STEFAN ZWEIG

'*The World of Yesterday* is one of the greatest memoirs of the twentieth century, as perfect in its evocation of the world Zweig loved, as it is in its portrayal of how that world was destroyed' David Hare

WAKE UP, SIR!

JONATHAN AMES

'The novel is extremely funny but it is also sad and poignant, and almost incredibly clever' *Guardian*

BONITA AVENUE

PETER BUWALDA

'One wild ride: a swirling helix of a family saga… a new writer as toe-curling as early Roth, as roomy as Franzen and as caustic as Houellebecq' *Sunday Telegraph*

JOURNEY BY MOONLIGHT

ANTAL SZERB

'Just divine… makes you imagine the author has had private access to your own soul' Nicholas Lezard, *Guardian*

ONE NIGHT, MARKOVITCH

AYELET GUNDAR-GOSHEN

'Wry, ironically tinged and poignant… this is a fable for the twenty-first century' *Sunday Telegraph*

KARATE CHOP & MINNA NEEDS REHEARSAL SPACE

DORTHE NORS

'Unique in form and effect… Nors has found a novel way of getting into the human heart' *Guardian*

RED LOVE: THE STORY OF AN EAST GERMAN FAMILY

MAXIM LEO

'Beautiful and supremely touching… an unbearably poignant description of a world that no longer exists' *Sunday Telegraph*

POPULAR HITS OF THE SHOWA ERA

RYU MURAKAMI

'One of the funniest and strangest gang wars in recent literature' *Booklist*

LETTER FROM AN UNKNOWN WOMAN AND OTHER STORIES

STEFAN ZWEIG

'Zweig's time of oblivion is over for good… it's good
to have him back' Salman Rushdie

MY FELLOW SKIN

ERWIN MORTIER

'A Bildungsroman which is related to much European literature from Proust
and Mann onwards… peculiarly unforgettable' AS Byatt, *Guardian*

FISTS

PIETRO GROSSI

'There is more power and pathos in this short piece of spare, timeless prose than in most densely-written novels' *Independent*

THE LIVES OF OTHERS

FLORIAN HENCKEL VON DONNERSMARCK

'Both a political document and an enduring work of art' John le Carré

THE THINGS WE DON'T DO

ANDRÉS NEUMAN

'A literary heavyweight' *TLS*

SIXTY-NINE

RYU MURAKAMI

'A light, rollicking, sometimes hilarious, but never senti-
mental picture of late-sixties Japan' *Library Journal*

SHUTTERSPEED

ERWIN MORTIER

'Beautifully elegiac… a remarkable novel' *Gay Times*